UNITED STATES OF SUCCESS

Brian Bonar

DEDICATION

Above all else, I dedicate this book to my parents who gave me life, my Brother Colin, Sister Moira Aunts, Uncles, and all those who surrounded me with love and support through the journey of life.

ACKNOWLEDGMENT

I acknowledge the experiences I have had. Those who wronged me from their actions, I learned compassion and strength. Those who guided me on my journey, those who set examples for me to follow, those who gave me positive guidance and support and above all those who have remained loyal to me in times of trouble and in times of success. After my father's passing, I was going through his pocketbook and found the following handwritten note he had to himself.

The true Gentleman is the man whose conduct proceeds from goodwill and an acute sense of propriety; who does not flatter wealth, cringe before power or boast of his own possessions or achievements, who speaks with frankness but always with sincerity and sympathy whose deed follows his word who thinks of the rights and feelings of others rather than his own and who appears well in any company a man with whom honor is sacred and virtue safe. Even if I achieve just 50% of the mantra, I will think I have served my Father well and my Innate Being in a way to be proud of.

TABLE OF CONTENTS

ABOUT THE AUTHOR

Brian Bonar – a Masterpiece in the Making

Life, like a beautiful mosaic, is created by a pattern of many pieces. It is only by stepping back that there is a clear vision of how each part complements and defines the whole picture.

Brian's complete story can only be told in the unique arrangements of how every experience, circumstance, and relationship has been pieced together to chronicle the creation of a lifetime's masterpiece.

By ordinary measures, Brian Bonar is a stunning success. However, as only the outside observers to his life's long journey, we are witness to barely the smallest portion of the whole story. In truth, the countless twists and turns that have defined Brian's timeline, like all rites-of-passage, have been arduous, demanding, and often taken him to the edge of human endurance.

As onlookers to the myriad of extraordinary accomplishments that Brian has achieved, it is like viewing an Olympic athlete's winning race. It's hardly an accurate accounting of the facts behind the success. As observers, we are not witnessing the seemingly endless hours of strenuous training, searing disappointments, and the singular test that challenges 'the self,' not in competition to others on the field, but rather to achieve the best from one's self. The greatest of all achievements, the real 'gold metal' is the triumph over the apparently endless trials and tribulations — seemingly against all odds, that has culminated in acquiring the hardest of all earned goals — a measure of self-mastery.

It is only by following Brian's inner, step-by-step ascent that the secret to his accomplishments is illuminated. By deeply understanding his inner core organizing principles, the answers are revealed. These inner driving forces expose the story-in-the story — going beyond a successful life to gain a lifetime of significant living.

The United States of Success offers his experiences as a calling to inspire others to achieve and accomplish beyond all inner limitations and outer obstacles — to never give up on the dreams that are yours alone. Brian offers his blueprint template for you to design the life you deserve to live.

To this end, Brian's life signature is to leave others in better condition than he found them. He has inspired and uplifted countless others on his journey — not as a handout, but rather as a hand up. Philosophically, his belief is based on an ancient proverb, "You can't help someone up the mountain without reaching the summit yourself." Brian states, "That in the end, it is not how much each of us has accomplished, accumulated or achieved, but rather, how many others will have benefited through our contributions that ultimately matters. This is the final report card of our life."

By peering into Brian's steadfast climb from inner triumphs to outer flourishing, what is revealed are three unwavering anchors — non-negotiable commitments to himself that have weathered the tests of time and trials. These core commitments have been central to defining his life's course, especially when all was without hope and there was no visible light on his path.

First and foremost, it all begins with his bedrock principle of trust. Brian states, "Trusting your inner wisdom as the primary source of guidance is number one. Trust life. It will support and guide you. Just listen to your inner voice; it always tells you the truth."

Trust engenders the ability to lead with integrity, openness, and consistency in every aspect of life. Brian affirms, "trust is the only true standard upon which to develop and grow. There is no second way. Without trust, there is no relationship with yourself or anyone else."

This unwavering commitment to trusting his intuition, even against all information to the contrary, has been the key to creating ever-expansive visions. Brian's resolute commitment to trust engenders his ability to spontaneously pivot—to revise, adjust, and course-correct on a moment-to-moment basis. Brian's shout-out is, "Trust, trust, trust yourself every step of the way."

The ability to see the apparently invisible to create the seemingly impossible—is the hallmark signature of every visionary. Brian's ability to see hidden opportunities obscured to ordinary eyes is his hallmark signature on countless projects. He has cultivated the skillfulness of a visionary by consistently going deep within and trusting his truth.

The second of Brian's core organizing principles lies in the ability to generate his own 'luck.' Brian defines this idea of luck as an ongoing process by 'taking charge of the life.'

Brian explains, "The power of personnel accountability is fundamental, as a way of life. There are no excuses. We are self-creating our future in every moment. Every one of our intentions, thoughts, and actions is constantly reflected back to us. We are generating the creation of our own luck — good or bad. Use every opportunity to learn and level up your awareness. This is an ongoing process — there is no final arrival, no ultimate endpoint. Stay alert to what you are creating for yourself!"

The last, and certainly not the least of Brian's cornerstones, is to fully and completely live with passion. To those who have had the privilege and pleasure to watch Brian in action report that he brings his 'whole' self' — authentically, genuinely to every aspect of his life. That there are no distinctions between business life, personal life, family life, or spiritual life... just one unified wholeness. All one, all the time, all in — fuels his passions, projects, and goals. Brian underscores, "Either you are all in, or you are not in at all!"

Brian drinks deeply from the cup of life and is ever aware of how time evaporates, no matter how ardently one attempts to stop the hands on the clock.

An erroneous belief perpetuates the myth that we have 'all the time in the world' left to do everything that has been put off into the future. The truth is that every moment is very precious. We cannot afford to waste even an instant on anything that does not contribute to our optimum well-being.

It is said that at the end of the game that the 'king and the pawn' go back into the same box. We are all gambling for more time. No one knows how much sand remains in our hourglass. Don't squander a second of this precious gift of life. Cultivate and nurture with great care that which you want to grow. You are the steward of your destiny. Invest your time wisely.

The chronology of Brian's path is a timeline strewn with celebrated successes and devastating challenges. This is life's curriculum—no one escapes this up and down rollercoaster. It is the process by which we evolve into becoming more valuable contributors and gain the wisdom required to reach back and help others up the mountains of life. This is the means by which the 'diamond in the rock' is polished into the brilliant gems that reflect the inner light of our true essential natures.

Brian reflects that without core organizing principles, we are like a boat without a rudder in a vast ocean—feeling like a cork bobbing on the surface of the ocean at the mercy of the wind, waves, and all other elements. Brian states, "Free will is our ability to do whatever we wish. However, in the end, we are all accountable for every action. The options are either life-enhancing investments or life-depleting choices?" Our futures are self-created. The power lies in our own hands. Stay the course, trust your intuition and live your life with passion."

For Brian Bonar, his masterpiece is not yet complete. It remains a work in progress. The United States of Success is a tribute to the unlimited possibilities that abide within each of us. It is the alchemy of passion, accountability, and the will to live both a successful and significant life that ultimately defines our unique masterpiece.

Set your sights high; the higher, the better.

Expect the most wonderful things to happen, not in the future but right now.

Realize that nothing is too good.

Allow absolutely nothing to hamper you or hold you up in any way.

— Ellen Caddy

INTRODUCTION

The road to success is paved with tests,

So you've got to believe in yourself above the rest.

Dream big, and let your passion shine,

If you don't, you won't end up with a dime.

Challenge the status quo, disrupt the market and say YES!

And remember that innovation is an endless quest.

Don't forget to change business for good,

If you want to change the world, then you should.

If you think with your head and listen to your heart,

I promise you'll get off to a flying start.

Make bold moves, but always play fair,

Always say please and thank you – it's cool to care.

Do what you love and love what you do,

This advice is nothing new.

Now, stop worrying about whether your business will be a hit,

Rise to the challenge and say, 'screw it, let's do it!'

~

Richard Branson's Poem to Entrepreneurs

If I were to describe my journey, I probably could not say it any better than Richard Branson's poem here. Behind the fancy cars, suits, and big houses, entrepreneurs go through rigorous journies to be successful. When I mounted the ladder to entrepreneurship, I honestly had no idea what I was doing. As a little boy, I was feeding my curiosity with different ventures starting from scratch. You see, when you come from nearly nothing, you barely have anything to lose. I mean, what lies beyond rock bottom, right? I think that is where my saving grace lay. In retrospect, I finally understand that things happen for a reason, whether we like it or not. We can either accept our situation or stay in denial about our struggle. The former will help you take the next step to fix your circumstances, while the latter leads to refutation and trying to put up a successful front and fool ourselves into oblivion. Either way, you have to take responsibility for your life because no one else will do it for you.

Let's try a little exercise. Take a pencil and a piece of paper and sit down in a quiet, comfortable place. Take a deep breath and think about your picture of success. Now, draw this picture on the piece of paper and reflect on where you are in life right now. How far are you from the image in your head, and where are you right now? If you are a considerable distance away, then this book is written just for you!

When I began writing this book, my main motive was to help all those struggling to get on the path of success. The crooked path ahead of you is a lot more than just that; it necessitates hard work and consistency, but the fruit you will get out of it will be worth the wait and the hours worth of sacrifice you will have to put in. The only question is, are you ready?

The United States of Success will take you on my journey from being the simple son of a shipyard worker to owning two businesses and everything in between. Your journey will be exclusively yours, but my point here is to take you through your rise and your fall, helping you hold on till we make it. You are not alone!

People often define success in a somewhat crude manner, even though the measure of purely materialistic means. A high-paying job, a mansion-like house, a fancy shiny car are all good to have, but they are, or rather, never should be the ultimate goal. Success is best defined through intangible means such as self-growth, learning, and maybe even self-actualization, et cetera, because directly linking success with tangible items means that you won't be successful anymore when you get to the other side because, well, what's next?

The best way to gauge and go about being successful is to have a purpose in mind, and then, your career, habits, and hobbies become the cause of fulfilling this purpose. As human beings, we need to do things to replenish the soul and not just feed the hunger for more inside of us. That also exists pretty naturally. But the important thing to realize is that the former will soothe you while the latter will make you hungrier for more. While wanting the best is probably the best motive, the inner desire should be your driving force instead of outer, worldly gains that will be replaced tomorrow.

We often wonder what the lives of famous and successful people like Jeff Bezos, Bill Gates, and TV sensations like Oprah Winfrey and so many other personalities are like, and what makes them so great. Although, once again, everybody's journey is distinct and unique in its way, what makes successful people well successful, is the constant effort and perseverance to get through the difficult parts of life to learn valuable lessons that will help them knock down hurdles in their way. It is the way you perceive a rock in your way.

You can either turn your car around because you can't find your way around it or find an alternative route to your final destination. Even if your progress and pace are slower than others, you will be way ahead of those who have never taken risks to get out of their comfort zones.

Philosophers and intellectuals have something to say about those stuck in the rat race of life, intending to accumulate more and more wealth to fit within the impractical standards of being 'successful.' In the words of **Buddha** himself,

"The only real failure in life is not to be true to the best one knows."

So, if you are looking to make more money or move into a bigger house, trust me when I say it will come as a means to an end and not an end in itself. While keeping up with an ever-evolving world is crucial to survive, keeping your values and belief system alive is also essential to stay content with life as you move forward. If you forget yourself in the process of being successful, whose definition of success are you even going for? Because the person you knew is long gone.

My story is for those who are not afraid to get down and dirty to pave their way to success. Success starts from within and while every step you take forward may not be in the direction you expect, keep in mind that perseverance and resilience will help you steer through the hurdles in your path.

Remember, you are the hero of your own story, and this journey is all about you!

CHAPTER 1:

ARE WE THERE YET?

Ironically, the first thing I will tell you before I take you through my story is the bottom line of a full life; no matter how bad you think you have it, someone else has it worse. And even though it does not change the way you feel, it does not really matter too much. What matters is how your feelings affect others. That's what matters most. And the only way you can affect others positively is when you become a positive influence in their lives by doing what you should have done in the first place.

My seventy-four years of life have been very long. So long that it almost reminds me of the famous quote by **T.S. Eliot** which goes;

"Life is very long."

I wonder what was going through his mind when he said that. He was not much older than me when his candle burnt out. Eliot was a smart man who had a life much different from mine, though. He was born in a wealthy family and had the liberty to do what he wanted when he wanted and whenever he wanted. His father did not influence or exercise control on him in any way, and he grew to be a successful, renowned man.

Today, I am the chief executive officer and chairman of two public companies. One of the businesses is all about green energy, soon-to-be a technology leader in the industry. Apart from that, I am also the co-owner of another sixty-four companies. I have always chosen to have a variety of business interests to keep abreast with the environment around me. It helps me make much more informed business decisions and keeps my mind running. So, you name it, and I have worked in pretty much every kind of business, such as the hospitality industry, coffee industry, and insurance industry. I have even expanded my interest in owning a plantation.

When I first came to the United States in 1984, I had a lot going on in my personal life. I had just ended a long-term commitment with my job and was expecting a child soon. Anyone in their sane mind would not have done something so unstable with a plethora of responsibilities on their head, but with a pocket half-full, I knew there were other great opportunities waiting for me so, I trusted my gut blindly and took a leap of faith. The journey to start afresh was so deeply embedded in my mind that I could not focus on anything else, and, finally, after several years of working hard and doing the right thing, I went to Alabama.

This chapter in my life really put a lot of things in perspective. It opened up my eyes to several experiences that I will always be grateful for. I found a startup in Alabama by the name of Quality Microsystems, which I helped go public. My experiences were leading into a direction that helped me practice my autonomy and gave me the confidence to keep moving forward. Of course, at this time, I was grateful that my decision to keep following my gut was materializing. Back when laser printers were the 'new thing,' I helped the company introduce a modern, two-thousand-dollar desktop laser printer.

The small accomplishment that started lining up gave me the courage and confidence to keep going. Shortly after I worked for Quality Microsystems, I got involved with another company, Laser Connection, where I introduced the concept of toner cartridges along with their laser printers. Basically, the product that we came up with was for a laser printer with a toner cartridge box with two-to-three thousand sheet ream of printing paper and called this a printer kit. This product performed so well in the American market back then that we ended up selling truckloads to clients and customers, scoring broad margins and exponentially increasing the revenue stream earned by this single product.

In my case, the first business turned out to be an experience, while the second was a source of practice. Once I had my foot through the door and slowly understood what the American market was about, I started to slowly propel in the right direction. My second company became so big that it expanded to Huntsville, Alabama, where I became an incubator for small businesses and startups. When I delved into my third business, my role was to develop and engineer resources and hardware for motherboards that would be placed inside printers. Things moved fast here, and the good thing about my adaptability was that I was moving along with the changes and because I also got to upgrade in the way things worked here.

My life, even at seven-and-a-half decades, never ceases to fail me. I have come to learn that change is the only constant throughout our human lives. As life progressed, so did I. From growing up to this very day, I have adapted to the changes around me. I grew out of broken relationships, the love of those around me, through grievances of lost connections and situations that were out of my control. Sometimes, the loss you experience strengthens you, while other times, it teaches you of your own capacity. However, what we often forget are the people around us. Life's hustle is always noisy, but we must remember the difference between white noise and the voices of those keeping us afloat.

I have always been the kind of person to go with the flow, and that is one quality that helped me change several roles, keeping me open to opportunities at all times. In the world I grew up in, you had to struggle to get up to where I am today, so I can safely say that I am a self-made man who wants to help others. I was lucky enough to have people in my life that took me by the hand and walked me through with them. But I also know that not everyone is fortunate to have someone to rely on, and hence, I want to be their voice of guidance through my words, experiences, and book!

The United States of Success is for *you!* It is for those struggling to achieve their definition of success. It is for the bruised, the broken, the hopeful, the hard workers, and most importantly, those that have a burning passion for doing something meaningful in their lives. When I was growing up, I was different than those around me, and I know there are many others out there who fall outside the mold of the 'perfect' human being and are learning to get there day by day. I want my story of success to be your story of success, so take away what you can and turn your life around.

You may not get the start that you wanted, but you can change your circumstances to end where you want to. I believe human beings have more power within the palm of their hands to take control of their situations. It all starts with a thought and the motivation to keep going, but you do get there. My life started when I was born in a poor family. I did not have many opportunities in my life except those that I turned to a challenge for myself and tried to look beyond.

Because I do not believe in luck, I think it was the energy that I gave off that attracted people and guidance in a way that would make me feel fulfilled. Because I have always been proactive and curious in nature, I grew up looking up to that one person who changed my life around. Frankly, I would say that he died too soon, but his calm demeanor, ability to handle difficult situations, and his practice to think outside the box always had me in awe. *How does he do that?* I would always think to myself when he would create solutions to his problems out of thin air like a magician pulls rabbits out of his hat!

Everything that I learned in my life has led me to where I am today. And I would owe it to all the people around me who taught me skills and still continue to do so to get here. Many times in our lives, we brush so many things aside so easily without paying any heed to them. For instance, how many times have you heard an entrepreneur say, '*I wake up at five a.m. and go for a jog when everyone else is asleep because it gives me time to plan my day ahead,*' yet there is only less than one percent of us who acts on this little piece of information. We listen to success stories and see how many dollars or pounds people have made at the end of the day, how sharply they are dressed once they get there, and how many places they have traveled on their Instagram and Facebook yet, more often than not, we forget where they came from. We conveniently leave out their journey and focus on the success and hope to God that life gives us the same opportunities as it did them. But I see that as people being short-sighted.

Opportunities are everywhere. As soon as you get outside of the box of financial viability, return on investments, time spent on creating blueprints, and our crude perception of failure, we realize that the chances all the wealthy people around the world took are right beneath our feet, too. It is just a matter of how sharp your sight is and how willing you are when it comes to grabbing an opportunity, even though it seems a million miles away.

What you do with your life is largely dependent on you. Most of us get caught in the rut to provide for families, following the safest route we know and have been taught, and never look elsewhere for our lives without realizing how much we are missing out on. As time revolutionizes, so do our opportunities and our path to success. If plan A does not work, move to B, and then C, and then keep going. Once you put your mind to a goal, submit your efforts in the same direction, and you will witness wonders happen for you. You will always move in the direction you put your effort in, and that is a fact. But remember, if you do not make an effort to change things around you, nothing will change.

Be it your personal or professional life, everything you want is within your grasp, but the key is to consistently go after it without the fear of failure because failure will come, but not to stop you, but to teach you to do things in the way that will get you the best results. And the most important of all is that you don't compare yourself or your position in life to anyone else's. Once you accept yourself, given your own strengths and limitations, you will be well on the way to figuring things around these hurdles and obstacles. Just so long as you keep your head high and your mind open to change and to learn, you will get where you want. It is often the start that is the toughest. And it is a proven fact much like **Newton's Law of Inertia**;

"If a body is at rest or moving at a constant speed in a straight line, it will remain at rest or keep moving in a straight line at constant speed unless it is acted upon by <u>force</u>."

Let's think about this statement for a second. What do you understand by it? According to my, I think this is one statement with the problem and the solution all-in-one. When you are in a state of rest, the first step always seems difficult. Once you consistently take one step after the other, you notice how your daily routine becomes somewhat doable, if not easy. The driving force to make your move is your willpower and motivation, which is decided by how much weight you put on the goal. It is always a good idea to fixate yourself and your vision on the goal. Once you have the first step figured out, everything else slowly starts aligning itself. For the train to get to its destination, the first bogey must be on track. If the last bogey falls off, the train still keeps going, but if the initial driver falls, you end up with an empty track. That is the difference between a person who has a lot of ideas versus a person who makes an effort to achieve their goal. And once you gain momentum, the process becomes easier, and if you keep at it, you find yourself in constant motion, and then it gets difficult to stop a person with a motive.

This law is not a coincidence, and neither is it a new discovery. The Law of Inertia exists as part of the universe, and it is when you start noticing it, you realize the order of things. Since we, too, are part of the universe, it is only right that we understand the way things work in order to keep moving forward in life. Once you give yourself that initial push to step up and start working, you will find yourself in a better spot early every day, learning and getting ahead of your 'yesterday yourself.'

Before I started my business from scratch, using my own two hands to put everything together brick by brick, I liked to think life put me on the path to acquiring as many skills as possible to be a boss, a leader, and most importantly, an entrepreneur. Once I got moving at the age of fourteen with my first business, I was unstoppable. I kept going because I wanted to, and I stopped at nothing. Everything big to small, simple to complicated, and ordinary to fancy; I had tried before I deemed myself qualified enough for my own business. I placed a great amount of trust in my skills, ability, and experience over the years and decided to jump headfirst into the situation I was put into, and after that, I went with the flow of the situation.

The business that I now call mine, Dalrada Corporation, was an already-established company back in 1982 that I took over in the mid-nineties. The company was bankrupt, and the shareholders were ready to liquidate the assets to protect their interests and investments in the firm, but I knew I had to do something to turn things around. If I had learned one thing over the past years, it was that things that are broken need to be fixed, not thrown away, because that does not solve the problem. Getting rid of what does not seem fixable only shows your ability to handle the situation and patch things up, and unfortunately, that is the problem with today's generation. Can't run a business? Sell it. Can't control an employee? Fire him. Can't find a solution to a problem? Abandon it.

I decided that the only way I could prove myself and save the company that I had invested in was to go down to San Diego and run the company in real time. I set my goal to rescue the organization and prepare it for take-off, and I did not budge no matter what situation arose after. I soon realized that I did not need a lot of money to run it because the only thing that needed to be upgraded was the management style and internal control. After that, I saw the fruit of my hard work right before my eyes as operations started to look up slowly. Ever since it has been up and downs, but never has a similar situation come into being.

Sometimes, I look at it the other way. What would have happened had I just shut down operations and manufacturing almost two-and-a-half decades ago? Well, not much. I would have started another business from scratch, fed my experience nice and healthy, and been a successful man today, too. But from the way I look at it, I have the privilege to say that I turned around and nurtured a business that was nearly in ruins. But I would be lying if I said I did it alone. I did have a few teammates and coworkers who helped me with their expertise and business acumen. I had to trust those around me, and being placed into a new environment was not easy, especially given that I did not know a lot of people involved in the business. Again, this required the utilization of my people skills and judgment of people to listen to valuable advice that would benefit the business while filtering out noise around me. In this part of my life, I slowly learned to depend on people and work collaboratively. It was also nice to receive those feelings of trust and respect in return that helped me build a rapport with my employees and subordinates.

Apart from a few of my employees, most of my task force has been with me for fifteen to sixteen years. I like to call this group of people my core team who have been there with the company and me through its good and bad times. My strategy has always been to maintain a positive, deep relationship with my employees. Not just because of how much they do for the company, but also because I believe they are deserving human beings, and trust and respect flow both ways. If I were in their shoes, I would want to be treated fairly and be understood when I need something. Apart from being a boss, my relationship with them also extends to humanity and dignity.

As a leader, I am always straightforward with the good and the bad performances at work, without crossing any boundaries of respect and hope for improvement. Once again, I am not a believer in simply getting rid of an employee if he or she has performed poorly. Being a boss, I hold myself equally responsible for their training and development as each employee is. My approach has always been to reward employees where their credit is due without them having to ask me for it. Taking the first step to make them safe has led my employees to feel appreciated, seen, and hence, they always do more than they are expected. And in my opinion, this is why they have stuck around with me for so long. The key is to build a two-way, functional relationship and see how the positive energy flows in synergy throughout the order of the company. At the experienced age of seventy-four, I have come to realize that all humans want is to be heard. And no matter how many machines live us, we will always need humans to function, and hence, it is advisable that we polish up our soft skills because those will take us far, be it at a job, in personal life, or even with ourselves. I have always treated my people as my biggest asset, and it really shows when people know they are valued. I don't think I have ever witnessed a Super Bowl game where an NFL team has all quarterbacks. You need a range of people and players on your team that will be your constant no matter how many new people come into the picture. As human beings, we need to pressingly focus on the power of good, healthy communication and comprehension, giving the people around us room to breathe and make sense of the situation. Just because you have a knack for something as a boss will not bring your team on board if you are not willing to openly bring everyone on board with you. You know what they say in Africa;

"If you want to go fast, go alone.
If you want to go far, go together."

If you were to ask me what has changed in my leadership style from back in the mid-nineties to today, I would say not much because all my strategies have been employee-centric, and people never go out of style. The best part is that I have decade-old payrolls attached to my company to present as proof. Your company will still manufacture, produce, and sell those goods, make those profit margins, and score those returns on investments, but the employees that will represent your company and your brand name cannot always be replaced. My aim had never, never has, and will never be about making money. Of course, making money is always nice because having money is important to survive and get by in an increasingly capitalistic world, but it is always a means to an end and never an end in itself. Money-making goals are short-sighted and never fulfilling. However, goals with a higher purpose of learning, growth, and making the world a better place always feed the soul and are bound to prosper in the long run. Keeping your eye on the bigger picture is the nail while staying motivated is the hammer that, together with the banging gesture, are bound to make things possible.

I, for one, find my motivation come from within while I see failure as a driving force that keeps me going. The inspiration that comes from within will never be replaced by any sort of extrinsic rewards or compensations, and neither is it enough to produce exceptional results for your employees. You can hire the best Human Resource team and acquire the best talent in the market out there, but if you fall short in keeping the employee happy, motivated, heard, and understood, soon enough, your hiring team will be posting online ads again for a position that was vacant just a few months ago. Not only is this a sign of bad leadership, but it also shows that the organization's weak culture is working towards selecting and recruiting good talent.

As long as you keep your human side alive – be it at work or on the street while driving – you are most likely to attract people who are human and humble, too. At work, I go the extra mile to make sure my employees feel at ease and like human beings around you and within the environment, you have created for them. Engage with your employees. Ask them important questions about themselves; if they are married or single? Where did they graduate from? What do they like to do during their space-time?

Do they have kids? Of course, there is a difference between a subtle conversation and being nosey. Your willingness to hold the relationship should dictate your stance on how much you should ask and how many questions are allowed per employee. The trick is to take it slow, start with basic questions every day, and make them know you genuinely care about them. Once the other person knows you are there for them as a boss and as a human being, you will see the appreciation and dedication come through all by itself. Come to think of it, there are only a few things you can control in life, and the way you treat people is totally up to you. So, treat them well, and it will be better for you. A motivated employee will give you a hundred-and-fifty percent back if you give them your hundred percent. But a demotivated employee will give you fifty percent in response to your fifty percent. That, right there, is the difference between a good and a bad boss.

"Take care of your employees, and they will take care of your business. It's as simple as that."

Richard Branson

When I was younger, I used to watch the Olympic Games with a lot of interest. I don't know what it was, but I was so intrigued to see the best of the best from every country just come together for a couple of days, showcasing the talent they have been working on for God knows how many years. It made me really want to put everything aside and give my undivided attention to these athletes. One of the most important lessons I learned about growth and progress was seeing athletes trying out the high jump back then and even now. Did you know? The high jump would only be about twelve feet back then, but now, it has come up to thirty feet! As insane as it sounds, people have practiced and practiced to test new limits. Players were stars, and when these same players became coaches, they really showed the world why they were the best to begin with. I find this growth amazing because it is based on sheer hard work and dedication, the two traits every human being is given to turn a life around!

As long as you keep in touch with your truest self, without getting overwhelmed by superficial luxuries in life such as fame, money, and wealth, you will keep your head in the game because you will not get lost in the noise. It is fairly easy to lose your way, many billionaires and entrepreneurs have lost everything in the process, but real success lies in never losing your true essence. And if you ask me, that is what has kept me motivated, and that is what makes me get out of bed with positive morale and do what I do every day consistently. I am aware of the energy and synergy in my control as I walk into work, and, hence, I try to keep myself motivated so it will wear off on my employees. You know what they say; positivity is contagious. We may as well use the good to our benefit and for the benefit of those around us.

I love being around my employees, coworkers, family, and even people as I walk down the street. Being surrounded by people makes me happy and hopeful. Listening to their stories, giving them my two cents on life and success is something I really enjoy. You cannot replace the human touch no matter what you do. Humans are hungry for the warmth of other humans. Period.

You put yourself inside an invisible box when you confine yourself to a certain setting, standard, expectation, and path. Today I see youth struggling with making money because they want to be happy, but the chase usually takes them so long that struggling and striving for more makes them dissatisfied to the point that even when they do have enough, they still want more. I don't encourage or condone superficial means of success. Money makes people happy, yes, but it is *never* the end goal! You will spend it. It will go away, and then what? Do you embark on another journey to make money from scratch? That's a vicious circle of life you are trapping yourself into.

The way I see things working today, personally, academically, and professionally is because everyone is talking about the way things *should be done*. As if there is some sort of equation you fit variables into, and a machine shows you an answer. Methodologies are set in stone, and ideas are a thing of the past, sending human creativity to garbage, limiting their most raw capacity and need to be free creatures, getting by through life, making their own mistakes, and setting their own standards for right and wrong. In my experience, this is not the way to go about life. All I see are parents worried about their children getting the right grades, going to a good college, graduating with a decent GPA, and landing a job with a multinational company where they are expected to work for years on a steady payslip. Sooner or later, these kids will burn out into tired individuals who are frustrated because they could not achieve so much in their lives. I see young individuals, aged thirty years or so, talking about how their life is over and they could not do as much as they wanted. I mean, look at me! I nearly started over when I was in my mid-to-late thirties, and I am still doing it today!

When humans make rules, they strip out the humanity of people and make the confinement box even stronger. Human beings are born as free, living, and breathing individuals. Some rules are healthy, but you cannot limit raw humanity and try to define it linearly. It is not that simple. I consider myself a successful man because I am free - free to do what I want, free to experiment, and free to speak my mind, try out opportunities, and connect with people.

Speaking of connecting with people, I remember back when I was working at IBM; I knew a guy named Jimmy Miller. He is one of those guys who really worked his way up the ladder by purely leveraging his basic skills, and that is why I admire him so much to this day. So, years ago, Jimmy Miller worked as an entry-level service guy, working over a typewriter at an old IBM table they had back then. But through the years, I saw this guy totally re-engineer himself into being the Plant Manager who everyone loved and admired.

I remember this one time when he was the plant director, and he would walk into a small department with maybe ten to twelve people on the line. He would ensure he knew who was working there. He knew the different roles people were managing. Some people were fathers who had kids. Others were sons looking after their parents, while others were wives managing different responsibilities. But Jimmy knew all of them. Before he would enter another department or room, he would gather information about the people there. And by that, I do not mean he would glance over their job descriptions and gauge their performance against certain set key performance indicators, no. He would just walk into rooms during his free time and speak with people to see how they were doing. He would talk to them about their lives, their kids, what they thought was interesting. I had always seen that guy surrounded by people, just laughing and discussing different matters with them.

There was this one time where he came over to me and started up a random conversation. I had not spoken to him a lot, but I knew who he was. Hell, everyone knew who Jimmy was!

"Hi, Brain. How are you?" He asked me with the same zeal in his voice that Jimmy was known for.

"Hi, Jimmy. Not too bad. You tell me," I replied.

"I was wondering when your son has his birthday. Next week, is it not?" He asked me, and I was lost for a second, wondering where he had heard it.

And the thing about Jimmy was that he was subtle, so it never seemed like he was prying or crossing any boundaries with everyone. If anything, people would expect to strike a conversation with him because of how charming he was at times. When Jimmy moved up the managerial ladder, people became happier because they had a boss they knew they could trust. If you ask me, he was a great businessman who made great career moves, and hence he landed the job he did, but he was good at it. He was never cunning or wicked or thought about throwing anyone under the bus for his own gain. He worked hard, he worked smart, and he worked right to get to where he wanted.

Earning the trust and respect of people is of utmost importance, and it is because he built that strong, two-way relationship with them is why he got people to be more productive. He knew he could count on them because he went the extra mile and did it for his employees, too. It always starts somewhere, and if you ask me, *the earlier, the better!*

One entrepreneur I personally relate with is Richard Branson for his humility and respect for other human beings. I have followed him and his work for a long, long time, and that guy never fails to impress me. Throughout his life, he has dropped golden nuggets for everyone to use as they deem fit. Maybe the similar age group draws me to his advice and life's lessons, or maybe it is just the fact that his guidance resonates well with me, but practically applying his life lessons has always borne me sweet, sweet fruit.

Out of his top ten success rules for entrepreneurs, the one that I most relate with and have applied to people from all walks of life, personal and professional, is to **Treat People Well**. Much like my personal experiences with Jimmy Miller and my Daddy John, I have personally experimented and experienced the difference between what people bring to the table when they feel appreciated versus when they feel unvalued. Once again, the comfort one human being brings to another, be it a boss listening to a pained employee or an uncle teaching the ropes of life to a nephew, you can have as much technological innovation on your side as you want, but at the end of the day, what a human being can do for you is never replaceable.

Kindness, empathy, and compassion will take you to new heights, build great relationships, and most importantly, teach you new values that you will cherish throughout your life. From great monks to successful entrepreneurs, everyone had the virtue of empathy in common that makes the world go round to this day.

CHAPTER 2:
TAKING THE PLUNGE

*"Learn from every mistake because every experience,
particularly your mistakes, are there to teach you
and force you into being more who you are."*

Oprah Winfrey

I was on the verge of tears when my mom came into my room bearing presents. It was my sixteenth birthday, and upto that point, all my closet was full of was either hand-me-downs that my mother managed to gather at thrift stores or outfits made from different cloth materials handmade by my mom.

"Thank you, mom!" I said to her, grateful and excited to find out what she had given to me.

"Open it up," she said to me with a smile on her face. I unwrapped a brown bag to find a beautiful black blazer, grey pants, and a pair of brand-new shoes. I was in tears. I hugged my mother and thanked her as much as I could. I still remember that day. I was happy and content with my life. Not that I ever complained about my life.

"I am the king," I thought to myself.

A person's teens are at a fragile stage in their lives. These seven years are when an individual starts learning about themselves by themselves. You will come to realize what makes you, you, and what your rawest, approximate dreams are. This is also when most of us fall in love and find out about our strengths. We start to make sense of the things around us and become receptive to our environment. We figure out our strengths and weaknesses. As human beings, we adopt what our parents and those close to us teach us when we are infants and toddlers. It is like our mind, which is clear like a mirror starts picking up habits that we mimic, but as we slowly go through our tender years, we use our building blocks to pick up other activities and habits that serve our most innate desires. In retrospect, I would say my implicit entrepreneur shaped my journey to who I am today. Of course, I was a curious kid, and back then, I had never thought I would be a CEO and a chairman of two public companies, but you know what they say, hindsight is 20/20, and looking back now, I realize how all my experiments and exploration have led me to be the man I am today.

Life is not fair, and that's probably the most definite truth out there. People are left behind in this race at different stages in life. Some start off below the threshold and always stay there, while others try their best to get out because they take those few steps out of courage and confidence and follow through with their heart. I think everyone has this courage within them, but unfortunately, sometimes the fear gets too loud for them to find their inner strength. You see, fear and courage are at constant war with each other. Your fear keeps you inside your comfort zone to protect you, while your courage helps you make a new comfort zone and allows you to outgrow it when the need calls for it.

I was born into a family where the man's fate was tied to the shipyard. My father had done it, and so had his fathers before him. And somehow, they had assumed I would do the same. Don't get me wrong, that is how I started. I didn't step back thinking, *'This is too embarrassing for me'* or *'I need to make more money.'* All I knew back then was that I had a burning passion inside me, and I did whatever I could to serve it at that time.

I first made up my mind about leaving the shipyards when I got accepted at IBM. The company had come to my town for the very first time, and I was excited to give it a try. The first time I applied, I failed. I thought to myself, *'It's okay, I will just try again.'* I knew in my heart that I could make it here, and I told myself that failure is just the first step towards success. I kept my head held high and applied once again, only to be rejected again, and again, and again, and before I knew it, I was applying to the same company for the thirteenth time!

I never knew what my life would be like if I didn't get into IBM because I was determined to get in. That is the mindset I have always worked with. Something that has proven to be true repeatedly in my seventy-four years is that perseverance pays off. Consistency is key, and as long as you have set your eyes on something, it will be yours if you just keep at it. And voila, after one plus a dozen applications, I got into IBM! I did not have any prior experience at a multinational company, and I surely did not have the academics on my side but what did help me was the skillset I had built all those years—leaving the shipyards was kind of like leaving a part of my family behind. In fact, I think I had even trampled over my dad's expectations of his son working with him to pursue what I really wanted to do.

"Please talk to this boy. He has a mental problem," my dad said to the doctor he took me to, Dr. Dougie Lyons, when I first told him that the shipyards were not the place for me and that I had gotten an employment offer from IBM. "You're off your head!" That is one of the first things he told me.

"What do you mean?" Dr. Lyons asked my father, looking at me and then back at him.

"He says he wants to leave the shipyards to work for IBM. Those people are crazy!" My dad says to the doctor. "These people wander about in white coats with a shirt and tie on."

The doctor hears my father out as he addresses his concerns. After my dad was done, he asked him to leave the room to speak to me privately.

"Son, your father does not understand the modern way of doing things," he told me. "Do what you think is right, and don't worry about your father. I will speak to him."

There was an unusual sort of assurance in Dr. Doughie's words. I felt like reassurance from an idealistic figure was what I needed was a push, and I got it. You see, Dr. Lyons was the doctor who brought me into this world. All eight pounds, and twelve ounces of me! After the doctor was done speaking to my dad, we went home and never spoke about IBM ever again. I felt like I was doing the right thing, and it turned out that I was. Sometimes, you just have to do what you think is right, and there is no other way around it. Yes, our parents gave birth to us, but it is also up to us to turn our lives around, whether they like it or not. You see, when you come from a family that was as underprivileged as mine, your parents usually make the decisions for you, and because you are desperately trying to make ends meet, you have extremely narrow ground to play and experiment with. However, if you responsibly keep going and believe in yourself, you will end up where you want to be. Of course, as I said, life is unfair, but it also depends on how you look at it.

You can either dwell on the fact that you have limited resources or accept your circumstances and work as hard as possible to change things for yourself. Either way, it all depends on you. It's like **Henry Ford** said,

"Whether you think you can or you can't,
you're right!"

Growing up, my brother and I always had to share a bed. My sister, however, was lucky enough to have her own bed. I am the youngest of three siblings. My sister is nearly ten years older than me, while my brother and I are only eighteen months apart. Our relationship with each other was fairly rocky, but I think that was because of our family dynamics in general. My sister has always been like a second mother to me, and my brother and I, though defensive of each other, had a love-hate relationship.

I remember this one time when my brother had some trouble with a few boys. We ganged up and protected each other, clearly putting out the message we were not a force to be reckoned with. My brother and I did nearly everything together. We played in the Boys' Brigade Band, where he was the lead drummer, and I was the bugle player. I was very proud of my talent, and all I wanted to do during this period was to win as many awards as possible. And once I put my mind to it, I saw my efforts manifest accordingly. I had my eyes on the Queen's award because of its prestige, I worked hard to one day achieve the award. When I did win the award, I was proud of my achievement, and best of all, the award was presented to me while my mother was presented with the Bible. That was the day I realized I had done something to make a difference in my life and that of my mother's.

We lived in a small town named to Greenock in Scotland in a small house where I grew up. I shared a room with my brother till he got married at the age of twenty-one. My sister, however, got her first-born privileges to a room all by herself. For food, my mother would often send me to the butcher shop after hours to find some leftover bones. These osseous fossils were boiled at our household to get the most out of them for our meals, and right after, my mom would enclose them in a newspaper so I could pass it to the next door neighbor till the bones had nothing else to offer.

Let me tell you a little bit about those around me as I was growing up. I was born into a family of three children, and we all lived in a house with three rooms, a small kitchen, and one toilet. We were a close-knit clan of five who liked to spend Friday night in front of the fireplace. Friday's were also bath days where we would get a chance to bath in the big, zinc bathtub that my parents had for us. And the thing is that because we would run on fixed resources, the challenge was using the same water to bathe in, and we would draw straws to figure out who would use the bath first, and the last person to bathe would get the dirtiest water. Even though today it sounds odd, it was pretty common practice, at least in the town I lived in. Everyone around us was pressed for basic necessities, but all I saw around me were people making the most of what they had and contentment with the simple life they had.

My mother spent most of her days taking care of us, disciplining us, and making sure everything in the house was in order. I was always fond of how hard my mother worked and how much she loved us. She would cook our favorite meals and do as much as she could even though we were living off of the bare minimum most days. But I never saw her complain to my father, and I guess that is where I get my patience and gratefulness from. Maybe it was because she was the oldest of five siblings herself. You know what they say about the first kid being the most compromising and understanding of them all. My mother, Margaret Murdoch, had three sisters and two brothers, and she was very fond of my grandmother. She always looked up to her, and although she did not speak much, I always saw her share everything with her mother. They both shared a twinkle in their eyes that I will always remember and hold close to my heart every time I think about either of them. It is as if my mother carried a part of her own mother inside of her, which was obvious in both their eyes yet magical at the same time. My grandmother, Mary Marshall, was almost mischievous but always laughed profusely. She was always a happy soul and had a positive influence in every room she walked into.

My grandfather was also a man of his own time. Jock Murdoch came from Glasgow and worked as a hairdresser, one of the most exclusive professions back then. He was a master barber and built a community around where he worked. All kinds of people in the town would visit him, and he made a good living out of his career. After my grandparents got married, they both moved to Greenock and lived there for the remainder of their lives.

When my mother passed away nearly twenty-five years ago, I was naturally upset, but I would like to think I was old enough to take the news. She had lived a good life, she was a good woman, and she knew her time had come. I remember she had a heart murmur that developed because of her old age. I had already moved to the United States when she had made it nearly to the end of her journey. She had a minor heart attack due to which her health weakened, and I was ready to come back to Scotland as soon as I found out. When my mother spoke to me, she promised me that she would get herself checked into the hospital the very next morning and made sure to convince me that she was going to be okay. She would often do that to make sure no one panicked because of her. My mother mainly kept to herself and tried to fight her battles on her own. A week later, as she was preparing to be discharged by a nearby medical facility, she passed away as she was sitting on the edge of the bed, preparing to leave. She had a major heart attack and had a blood clot in her heart, whose chaos she gave into, losing the battle against her own death.

I still feel my mother with me every step of the way. I know some of you might think I am probably nearing my own days, but I know I feel her presence around me. Her soft aura, gentle grace, and warm presence surround me and are still a source of inspiration for me. In my experience, which we have once loved, always find a way to stick around in our lives. If not physically, their memories, thoughts, and recollections are always there.

My father, Henry Bonar, married my mother when he was twenty-one years old while my mother was twenty. He was a small guy who stood on a frame of five feet and seven inches, who came from Greenock. One of his greatest qualities was how calm and collective he was, no matter his surrounding circumstances, and I put a considerable amount of weight on that positive quality of his. God knows patience does not come easy, but he carried his composure fairly well. He never hit us, yelled at us, and never even fought with my mother. If anything, he always guided all of us and then backed off so we could make our own decisions and learn from our mistakes. His insightful nature made him approachable and a likable guy, even though he was not social, and neither did he mix with a lot of people. From all I remember, he was a hardworking guy who would spend a fair amount of time away from home, trying to make a decent living for his family.

My father did try to offer me his two cents after I went through my second divorce. He told me that I was involved with too many women. "Son," he said. "Your mother is the only person I have been with in my entire life. And I know for a fact that there is nothing like it out there. You, Brian, are too confused. You don't know what you want, and that is not how relationships work," and in retrospect, he was not wrong.

My father passed away a mere ten years after my mom did in his late eighties. When he was alive, he was just like a corpse because he did not talk much or interact much. He slowly wasted away, and on most days, my siblings saw him go to bed clutching the little teddy bear my mother had given to him. She was the love of his life, and he could not keep away from her.

When we were much younger, my father went to Canada for two weeks to visit his family for vacation.

When he came back, he spent enormous time with my mother. I clearly remember asking him how his trip was, to which he replied, "Everyone there is great, but I am never ever going to be away from your mother again." That is when we knew she was the love of his life and his soulmate.

Before my dad passed away, I was fortunate enough to spend some time alone with him because he had told me he wanted to spend some time with me. It gave me a chance to reconnect with my old man and reminisce about all the old times we had together.

"I thought you did not know about that," I said as I made yet another confession to him about the shenanigans I was involved in as a kid.

"Son, I know everything you have done in your life; I am your father. The only person you were fooling was yourself. When you are doing things you know you should not be doing, you think you are clever enough to dupe everyone around you, but you are dead wrong," he said laughingly.

I remember probably the only time I had seen a reaction from my father. One day, he woke up and picked out his usual morning paper, which happened to have his picture, for a generous act he had carried out, one which I cannot mention even right now because of what he told me that day. He went down to the newspaper publication and told them off royally to publicize his picture without his consent. He came back, frustrated and boiling, fuming and pacing all around the house. I took my chance and decided to ask him why he was so riled up about the whole situation.

"Dad, why are you upset? Isn't it a good thing that you have your picture on the paper? People know you and know the good you have done," I asked him, as innocently as possible, making sure he does not get more upset.

"Son, I do what I do for me. My acts are not for people to think that I am some wonderful, special person. I am not looking for acknowledgment from anyone else. I don't need notoriety," he paused. "I need to have the ability to wake up every morning, and as I look at myself in the morning to shave, I should be able to see Henry Bonar and be happy with it. That's all that I want."

As if I was not impressed with my father already, his words caught me like a deer in the headlights. I realized once again that day that my father is a down-to-earth, wholesome man who is secure in the way that he is. This man is not material despite his potential; he is not greedy and is certainly not worldly. When I see this man who is the embodiment of Henry Bonar, I see a satisfied, grateful man who wants peace and contentment out of life, and my respect for him grew even more. The happiest people in the world that you will come across are those who make the most of their circumstances without questioning, complaining, and comparing their lives with those around them. I can see the values of my parents reflected in many tasks I carry out in my daily tasks, and for that, I will always be grateful.

After I spent that time in Scotland, I had to take a business trip to Korea. This was the time that he had passed away, and, unfortunately, I could not make it in time to say goodbye to him, but I am grateful yet again that I spent an ample amount of time with him before he left.

"Son, I am going to go soon," he said one day we sat down. "You don't need to come back for me if you ever decide to do so. If you ever think there is a need, come back for your brother and sister because they need you." These were probably his last words for me; to value the people around me: my family, my blood. My brother had called me before the service and told me that they had to put my father away in the preceding days or we would have to wait for another week, and I was not going to have my father wait because I could not find a flight back in time from Korea to Scotland.

I told my brother that he should do whatever he needed while I tried my best to get to my father, who had been in a coffin for two days now, in time. I never made it to the ceremony, but my family told me that over a thousand men lining on the street the day of his service had come to just pay tribute and their respects to him. According to what I heard, more than a fair majority of those people had never been seen around my dad, but it felt like they had known Henry Bonar for ages. That day I realized that although my father looked like a small, petite man, he was really a giant who made a difference in the world. And indeed, whatever he did was not for himself but for others.

My siblings and I had an on-and-off relationship as we were growing up. My brother Colin Niven Bonar and I were two peas in a pod. Don't get me wrong, we had our ups and downs, but it was always us against the whole world. About five months ago, I received the unfortunate news that my brother had passed away from a dreadful accident. He was blown off his feet, and he cracked his skull as he landed on the asphalt sidewalk.

My sister, Moira Bonar, was quite a few years older than me, got married to a man named George, and settled in the same town as she was born. In fact, she lived in a house just about three miles away from the house we were born and raised in. She gave birth to two daughters, and they all lived in Greenock until my sister died of breast cancer about twenty years ago.

One of the biggest influences in my life was my uncle, who I called Daddy John. I would spend hours with him during the week and often on weekends. If I were to give credit to someone for my business acumen, it would be my Daddy John. He was a man of a few words and many ideas, always finding a solution to problems, bridging the gap by identifying a need to issues, and in the meantime, also earning enough for the family. He took me along on many expeditions that taught me nearly everything I know today.

I was never the best at school. In fact, every day after I would get off, I would meet Daddy John, where my daily expedition would start. At the age of fourteen, I had already left school and joined the shipyards, which, as I had mentioned, was the fate of nearly every boy in the town that I lived. At first, I was assigned to the boilermaker's shop. Here, my job was to collect money from nearly five hundred workers and get them a hamburger bun that had butter on it. Two weeks into the job, I was done because I was thinking of another way of doing things. I think I just got instinctual at this point because something had clicked in my head, and I went to my mother.

"How much does a roll cost?" I went over to her and asked, knowing very well she would know what was brewing in my little head.

"All rolls cost five pennies, Brian," she told me.

"And how much does it take to butter a roll?" I asked her.

"I don't know, two pennies?"

I thought about it for a while, and in the meantime, the equations just filled my head on their way to help me make a decision preceded by a question.

"So, why am I paying the baker fifteen pennies when I can do the same and make some money?" I asked as I recognized this as an excellent opportunity.

"Son," she said to me. "We are working-class people. We do not know how to conduct business. You need to stay content with your situation, and life is going to be good for you."

I paused for a second as I contemplated on her words, but I finally decided that I was not going to take it. "Mom, I cannot do that. I have to do it!" I told her, once again, gently but assertively.

And that is when my true entrepreneur was born. I believe that although I did pick up on some of the habits of my Daddy John, it was also second nature for me to see a good business opportunity and take advantage of it, and so I did as much as I could.

Unfortunately, I also had to say goodbye to my Daddy John, along with so many family members. But life and death are something we have to accept at the end of the day. I know it is much easier said than done, but at the end of the day, life goes on. We are all walking on a tight rope that will only get tighter and tighter as we get closer to the end, till it snaps! However, with our limited time here, we can try to make the most out of our opportunities and leave a legacy behind that will keep us alive for generations.

Although Daddy John was my mother's sister's husband, Aunt Polly and Daddy John were like an extended part of our family. We were all very close, and there was barely any time that we went on without seeing each other for more than a day at a time. We would have supper together, and in my view, we were not a family of five but a family of eight. Even though my dad and Daddy John did not speak much, they always seemed to connect when we all got together.

Daddy John's death makes me immensely sad, not just because he died but also because had he been attended to earlier, he probably would have lived. Now you see, back then, when I was still a young boy, we did not have cellphones or even landline options except if you are in a corporate setting, but we did have a family signal. For dinner, when one family had scraped enough for a feast, they would hang a mop out a window and that was the house where everyone would gather, and we would eat. However, for emergencies and other such events that needed immediate help and attention from others, the house in need would stick out a broom.

One day, when I was walking back to our home, I saw a broom hanging out of Daddy John's house, and I immediately ran inside. I ran up the stairs to see Aunt Polly panicking while Daddy John rolled on the floor in pain. I stayed with him while my aunt ran to the neighbors to ask for some help to go to the phone box and call the ambulance. I cradled my Daddy John to make sure he felt at ease because I did not know what was coming next.

"Brian," he said. "Take care of your Aunt Polly for me and make sure she is okay." Those were the last words out of his mouth before he finally passed away in my arms right in front of my eyes.

Losing someone is devastating, and little did I know that Daddy John's death was the first of many I was going to have to face. But so many years down the line, as I stare down the barrel of 'the gun' myself, I realize that life is going to end anyway. For me, for you, and everyone else around you. But the most you can do is be good to each other, treat each other with respect and kindness, and learn from your surroundings. I have realized the importance of giving back as much as you take because life is a two-way road. You cannot just take because then there will be an imbalance in your life, and similarly, you cant just give because then you will be empty. The goal and the challenge are to surround yourself with people that vibrate at the same frequency that you do so you can see eye-to-eye with like-minded people.

My mother, father, siblings, Daddy John, and even Jimmy Miller will always be with me because of the way they treated me and vice versa. Creating an impact in life is highly important because all we have is each other in a world that is a shark tank.

I strongly believe in life after death and that we will live life even better than the one we have. But while we are here, we need to find an equilibrium between our purpose in life and life's purpose for us. Of course, you will learn this as you go because it took me nearly seven-and-a-half decades to get where I am today, in a position to be sharing my own wisdom with you. You will lose your way, and then you will find it back, but as long as you have a laser-sharp focus, you will be better off after life throws a few curve balls at you.

To this day, I see myself as someone who is self-taught and took every opportunity that came my way. I would make sure to occupy myself in all sorts of things. Even if it was something I did not know, I did not back down from learning the process. All my hands-on experiences helped me get ahead in life, looking past the difficulties of the situation.

In 1984, I finally got a chance to go to the United States – the land of opportunity, and start a new course of life there. I did not have much, just about $2,000 and a pregnant wife, and all I could think at this point was that I needed to make it here. I saw the opportunity as a fresh start and started to look for jobs immediately. My wife did the same because we were running out of money since we were running on savings. After a few days of looking, she landed a job as a receptionist while I filled out an application for a company in Mobile, Alabama.

This job was another challenge for me since I had never been to Alabama in my whole life. Due to various trips through IBM, I did get a chance to visit the US often, but the one state that I had never been to was on the path of a new journey I had just come across. I did not know how I was going to do the job, but all I did was take a leap of faith and try out my luck once again.

I saw everything that I did as a child manifest in many different ways as I grew up. From being a quick thinker to a risk-taker to an entrepreneur, everything I have done since my early childhood made me into the practical human being able to focus in tough situations, spearheading my way to look for a solution. And the more I saw the fruit of my efforts ripen, the more I wanted to move forward to enjoy the benefits... and so, I kept moving forward and continue to do so!

CHAPTER 3:

THE MENTEE-SHIP

My Daddy John had always been my *'ride or die'* as I was growing up. We were like Batman and Robin, but he probably never knew that. It is odd sometimes, even uncanny when I think about it right now. Everything that I am today probably started ages ago when I was about 14 or so, waiting for school to end so I could go and meet my Daddy John, my uncle, and join him for the many adventures he would set out for every day.

I remember this one time he had purchased two boats by the shipyard that needed repair and restoration. *'A new escapade,'* I thought to myself as I met him that day after finishing up my classes for that day. We had a common meeting point where he knew I would meet him every day, and he would wait for me. Back then, it was not like today. We did not have cellphones, but we did have the time and patience for each other, and sometimes, that is what I miss the most about being a young boy. However, I am grateful that I was able to drown other sources of noise and distraction than to grab every opportunity possible.

The idea behind getting two boats was also two-pronged, which I would find out later. We spent hours fixing the boats by the dock, and as I recall, I would actually enjoy doing so. After days' worth of efforts, we finally finished fixing the boats, and it was time to sell them, but that's when Daddy John told me what he really had in mind.

"Well, what do you think?" I asked Daddy John as we both stood at the dock, looking down at the boats that had now been restored.

"They look sharp. Good job, Brian!" He said to me.

"So, are we going to take them back to the place we got them?"

"Why would we do that?" He asked me.

"Well, I thought we would sell them back and get money for our services and efforts," I told him in an oh-so-obvious tone.

"Haha, come on, Brian. We are not going to do that with both the boats," he slightly chuckled at my confusion.

"You see, I always try to think of more than one way of return on our investments."

"Okay? So, what now?" I asked him, eager to know what was going on in his mind.

"Well, you see. The money we make for the repairs on the boats is going to help us buy the first boat for ourselves. This way, we have bought an asset in our names. This is going to be our security blanket.

Do you understand?" I took a few seconds to absorb his words and then nodded at him, waiting for him to continue what he was about to say.

"Then, we will sell the second boat, and that will give me enough money to buy your aunt the fur coat she has been asking me for," he finally revealed to me. Once again, it took me a second to join the dots, but when I eventually understood his thought process, it made sense to me. He was an opportunist! His mind worked like a football field where the attacker had to improvise the situation at hand to match an inflow of defenders right before scoring a goal. I was intrigued, and at that moment, all I could think was, '*I can't wait to learn more!*'

However, as expected, we did run into a little bit of trouble. The second boat that we spent many hours repairing, unfortunately, sank to the bottom of the river, beside the dock it was moored on. Just a few days before we were to sell it, a huge storm hit, and all we were left were with the remains of the very instrument we had fixed in the recent past. However, my hope reflected that of Daddy John's in that we both did not give up and instead managed to get some help to pull the boat out of the water and began working on it from scratch. Thanks to teamwork, in no time, the boat was good enough to be used and launched into the water and was sold, and we reaped the fruit of our hard work.

"We are going to call this boat Apache," Daddy John told me. "Because it has a patch on the side of it."

We were working on the finishing touches of the boat when we named the boat right before we sold it off.

"Apache. I like it," I smiled at him.

Daddy John was the guiding figure in my life that I did not know I needed. My father was working around the clock all the time to feed four mouths at home, leaving for work at 6 am each day and returning at 8.30 pm. Needless to say, he would be too worn out by the time he got back to be able to fully give his family the undivided attention we needed, and we all understood his role in our life. No one complained but felt his absence in our lives in order to keep us sheltered, clothed, and fed.

The way Daddy John operated was different, strange, but interesting. As opposed to spending long, hard hours to make ends meet, he would spend a fixed amount of dedicated time working his job till 3 pm, and then he used to spend time till 8 pm working on different business ventures where I would go along with him. One thing I learned during those times, thinking back, is that no matter how tired or exhausted Daddy John was, he kept going until he succeeded. And when things did not go his way, he would always alter his methodology, but, at large, he kept his eye on the target and never went astray. That is where I would like to think I got my determination and business acumen, two qualities that have helped me be the man I am today.

If I were to define my uncle in one word, I would say he was perceptive. Sharp when he needed to be, empathetic when the situation arose, and astute, getting things done without an excuse or fear of failure. He was a smart guy that did not speak as much as he observed. Being a young boy in this world is tough and was even tougher given my situation, but I did get by with a little help from my Daddy John and his tactics to get by. His strategy was always the same; *ready, set, achieve!*

Entrepreneurs who have a wide-eyed vision always benefit from the opportunities around them. You see, I am a believer in the fact that everyone comes across multiple opportunities in life, but the only challenge is that the window to grab this chance is narrow. In fact, this shot is tapering so fast that it will almost always disappear if you do not consider it on the spot. Given the fast-paced world we live in, we have to be on our toes, reaching our hand out, or we will be sped by without even realizing it.

"There is no box you can fit yourself in," Daddy John told me one day. I was too young to understand what he meant, but I kept my eyes and ears open. I often did that. It took me years to understand his wisdom, but with a little faith in his words and trust in his instincts, my younger self was able to follow through with his direction, often realizing his sagacity as I would retrace my steps through the process. But you know what they say, right? *Hindsight is 20/20.*

Human beings have the tendency to build boundaries and protect themselves within 'comfort zones,' halting the process of achieving their own potential to the fullest. Learning from Daddy John's experience, I have come to realize that the bigger, thicker, and fancier your boxes, the more likely you are to stay inside them. This is great if you want a steady, predictable life and your personality is that of a conscientious person. However, if you know you have the burning passion of an entrepreneur inside of you, even those that are 'by the book' need to push themselves beyond the mental, emotional, and physical borders they set for themselves. As long as you keep your eyes and mind open, you will move forward. Of course, it goes without saying that you will not be successful at everything you do, but everything you try is going to successfully teach you your strengths and weaknesses.

There was this one time Daddy John had randomly – as per my standards – decided to purchase a hundred chickens nearly three months before Christmas. He would take care of them, feed them, water them, and make sure they grew big and healthy, for he had a plan to sell them right before the big event for a profit in exchange. However, after months' worth of care and dedication, he found out that the customers he was selling to did not want live chickens. Daddy John, as we knew it, did not stop there; he took the highway and made sure that his effort did not go to waste. And voila! The season's greetings were even sweeter for him as he made sure everyone had chickens the way they wanted them. In a matter of time, he learned to kill and pluck the poultry birds in time to make the profit he wanted out of them before time ran out.

Keeping a steady pace is of crucial importance in life. I will probably sound like a broken record when I tell you, *'Consistency is key,'* but take it from someone who has tried and lost and then succeeded; it works! And if you fall down, it is totally okay. Take your time to feel your defeat but don't let it hold you down because you will want to take a break sometimes, but the problem becomes worse when you dig yourself so deep into your failure that you begin to lose your way back. If there is anything guaranteed in life, it is change, and there is no other way around it. It is up to you to figure out how far you are willing to go, equipping yourself with the armor of learning and experience to make things right.

If I were to put it straight, nothing would come to you easy. Sometimes, you will have to put yourself out there, and other times, things will come to you for the energy you put out to the universe. Either way, perseverance, and persistence will take you on fun, and interesting rides in life, with enjoyable return on investments people, will be able to learn from. When you hustle using your basic, innate skillset, you get to learn about yourself through hands-on experiences. I have put myself through many different roles, and it began with me using my hands as tools when I did not have the experience. One of the little ventures I started when I was much younger was when I bought a fish tank and got tropical fish to breed and sell them at a profit. Although I did not make a lot of money out of business, I was already considering myself a businessman, and the next time I dive into something similar, I would already know a few small things about running a small venture to begin with. The point to note is that it does not matter the size of your steps as long as you keep moving forward.

"No matter how many mistakes you make or how slow you progress, you are still way ahead of everyone who isn't trying."

Frederick Douglass

When I started the business out of serving the boilermakers their daily hamburger bun with butter, I was determined to prove a point not only to myself but also to my mom. I knew she asked me to stay content for a good life ahead, but a part of me was motivated enough to scratch that 'entrepreneurial itch' I had no idea I had back then. But once I got the ball rolling, I felt I was unstoppable. Within ninety days of running my first business at the early age of fourteen, I had earned enough to buy something for my family, which was a huge deal back then; a black-and-white fourteen-inch television set that showed only one channel back at the time, which was BBC One.

Before I completely bid farewell to the shipyards, I was serving time to work on my apprenticeship. Here, I was working on the engines of various boats and the functioning of their motors. Every day, it was working about the amazing chemistry between oil, water, and other lubricants that make these boats work efficiently. One fine day while I was carrying out my regular tasks, an idea popped into my head. I decided to go to a friend of mine to share my proposition, which would help us gain a new set of skills as well as some money on the side.

"Hey, so I was thinking. Why don't we work over the weekend to provide basic car services to, initially, our friends and families?" I told him.

"Sure, I mean, why not? What do you have in mind?" He asked me.

"Well, I think we can offer oil changing services and pick up on other similar solutions for some extra cash."

"Sure, we can start it and see how it goes," he told me, and from then on, we did not just offer the services we had discussed, but we ended up self-learning multiple techniques, for instance, changing spark plugs and eventually, we ended up making enough money for me to afford a car.

One day, my dad and I were working when I struck a casual conversation with him. This incident took place after I had broken the IBM news to him, so needless to say, we were not exactly best friends, but I did not sense any animosity coming from him.

"Dad, I am going to build my own house in Gourock," I told him. Gourock was three-and-a-half miles from where we used to live and were brought up.

"You need to rethink your decision. I think you have amnesia, son," he told me, quite obviously displaying his disappointment in me.

I knew where this was going, but I kept my calm because I wanted him to understand that this is an act of trying to grow and not rebellion.

"Dad, I am going to be fine," I told him. "I am building my own house to sustain myself." I had seen my brother-in-law do the same and I was determined this is another thing that I absolutely wanted.

I will never forget my humble beginnings because they make me who I am. My mother had exactly two pots that she used to cook us our meals in her little kitchen. No matter what our circumstances were, I had never seen my mom complain or rant to my father about the way her life was. It was as if she had dedicated all her time to us, and the same goes for my father. He found a small plot of land across from the house we used to live in and put up some plants out of which we used to eat. Everything we ate was produced locally and organically. That is all we could afford back then, and we were content with what we had.

I remember Sundays and the feast we used to have together as a family. This is where Daddy John and Aunt Paulie would often join us and share the meal that my mom would make. Sunday was church day, and for dinner, my mom would cook roast beef with deep-fried potatoes, also known as roasted potatoes. She would fat fry them in her only pot till they were completely done. The thought of that dinner still makes me hungry. It was one of my favorite dishes ever.

My mother cooked quite a few square meals for us. She tried her best to give us the best life she could. She would discipline us, or try at least, and keep everything in the house in order. My father would work all day and night, so she could hold up the fort. As a family, we spent all our time in the same house and made many wonderful memories that I will cherish forever. If you ask me, the man I am today is deeply rooted in my house back in Greenock.

I remember I had a neighbor when I was growing up. His name was Jimmy Tomlinson, and although he was a quiet guy who never spoke much, he had a vivid mind and spoke through his paintings. He would make watercolor paintings and wrote Scottish poetry in his little house not too far away from ours. Jimmy would also write plays that were then reenacted in the local town theatre. He was a well-liked guy because of his many talents, and I admired every one of his skills, especially because he had worked to acquire them on his own. I was fascinated due to how perfectly he took up these talents and worked on them to perfection. Years before he passed away, I went to visit him one day. We had an on-and-off relationship and would make small talk every time we ran into each other. I remember entering into a house that had beautiful paintings on every wall. And the place for sure looked like it was owned by a painter given how colorful it was, with paints and art supplies all over the place. In today's time, I would call him modern-day Di Vinci.

Little did I know, Jimmy had something for me, too. A little while before he passed away, he handed me two paintings. I was always a fan of his work, but I had no idea Jimmy had something in store for me. One of the paintings was a print from an old newspaper. I decided to take it and get it framed just to preserve the memory of my neighbor. What I loved about Jimmy was the use of colors and their chemistry in his paintings. He would perfectly stroke a brush to paint the sky a bright blue yet make subtle, beautiful clouds as if he knew what the portrait needed without giving a second thought about it. I absolutely adored his hard work, passion, and dedication to serve his painter, writer, and poet itch. Another painting that he made for me was that of a farm, yet again using beautifully blended watercolors to depict a picture of the scenery as perfectly as God had created it. I was in awe! This was the same farm I had bought in the hills behind a town called Paisley that was being renovated. I have preserved the two paintings in the memory of my dear friend and neighbor to this day to honor his hard work and dedication.

Even though it has been nearly thirty-five years or so since he passed away, I still remember him richly because of the kind of person he was. He left his legacy behind for us to remember him without saying many words and was remembered by people in my birth town long after he was gone. This silent mark is what I loved about Jimmy so much. He left the world but also left behind a heritage that he is still known for.

I think it is immensely important that we as humans network our way through life. Human beings crave personal intimacy and social touch, and there is no second to that. Richard Branson talks about the importance of creating a network for yourself as you excel through life. He highlights the need to know your surroundings and always to stay rooted in where you come from. Unknowingly, I was following Richard's advice even as a kid. Who knew I would run into someone similar to me in terms of their belief systems and ideologies. Back then, I made connections by getting to know people, working for them, being around them, and simply striking conversations with them based on similar likes or interests. That is something I advise everyone I come across to do. It does not really matter if you have a lot in common with someone because staying in touch with people with a difference in opinion most definitely keeps your mind open to other ideas but as long as you view their opinions objectively, you should be able to have healthy conversations with all sorts of people. Your network does not need to have all like-minded people. It is not about hanging out with people you like. You might hate the way someone does something, but they might actually be aiming to do something really good. That's okay as long as the end result is positive and it helps you learn and grow.

It is much easier to get in touch with your idols and mentors these days. Someone you aspire to be is just the click of a button away, and even though sometimes it might take a while to get to them, but as long as you keep at it, you will get there. Always remember, *your network is your net worth,* and no truer words have ever been spoken! To young people out there reading my book and following my story, I have combined a few tips and tricks to get out and about. Making ourselves known may very well be necessary for us in the few years to come if we are indeed chasing our definition of success. Once again, remember perseverance and persistence are key!

Rule #1

Socialize! Socialize! Socialize!

I cannot emphasize enough how important socializing is but in a healthy space and manner. No, this does not mean that you have to attend parties at every nook and cranny out there. Start subtle but do it. Attend events taking place relating to the industry you are interested in. If you are a marketeer, look around and find the hottest events around you. Be present virtually, physically, or socially – whatever floats your boat and makes you feel safe but be there. It does not matter what your personality type is. Introverts need to be around people as well. Hell, Daddy John was a big, big introvert, but he chose his crowd by scouring the people around him and making contacts and build networks that served him, but for that, he first put himself out of his comfort zone and took the plunge.

Similarly, you will first need to do some research. Gauge people, engage with the audience, and maybe even run some elevator pitches to deliver your personal brand. But as long as you keep trying, you will stick in someone's mind. No one makes it through in a smooth, scratchless way. Everyone learns and grows in a trial and error manner. And remember, the more you put yourself out there, the higher are your chances of being spotted. What is that thing statisticians say about probability?

The more contacts you make, the further you can actually go because if someday you need help and look back, you will have someone from your network help you out, and this is how you will start forming stronger bonds by giving and taking. Trust me when I say this; there are not all bad people out there. Many people I came across were willing to help me when I was at my lowest. All I tried to do was sound confident and sure of what I wanted. People dig that kind of energy because people who believe that good will come to them often find themselves surrounded by this goodness and positivity. Sooner or later, it always comes!

Rule #2

Your communication skills are your most important asset.

Quality over quantity! Choose what you say, rehearse your words, and boom! You will be out there leaving people with little golden nuggets they will remember for the rest of their lives – *or probably not.* But that's also fine.

Over here, I would like to add that it is not *all* about what people think. You are always going to have haters as you move along who will try to bring you down. But the task is to keep your focus laser-sharp on those that will lift you up. When you are out there getting things done, it is barely ever about your level of expertise, and especially when you are starting, it is about getting the job done. Quite honestly, this threshold will get you through. You are much more likely to get replaced by someone who gets the job done and is not afraid to roll their sleeves up and get down to the job than someone who has extensive experience but only does things halfway. Keep your eye on the bottomline, which should be: keep moving forward and putting in the effort. The money will come, the car will come, and the fame will follow for sure, but these are never motivators to keep you going. Keep your headstrong and feet grounded. It is okay to aim for the stars but make sure you never lose your balance.

There are so many workshops and online courses you can take online to work on your communication skills if needed. Google up what is going on around you and make sure to keep trying things out to stay in touch with the direction in which things are moving. It is not about the size of your boat but the motion you can create in the ocean. The trick no one ever tells you about is that you are supposed to get through life learning at every stage. Sometimes it is the people around us that teach us, while other times, it is you who will learn first hand. Either way, you do not get a manual of step-by-step items you need to accomplish in order to move forward. This is real life, and you are only handed down an itinerary or a script when you are acting. And to be your most authentic self, you have to let go of all the drama and face the music, or you will be a puppet for the rest of your life.

Once you start working on yourself, you will see things work out for you. It is like a domino effect, and the only thing that stops a good causal sequence is a break that is too big to keep the flow going. Have some faith in yourself and your intuition which will help you cruise through most situations. During this digital age, things are more nimble and even more so approachable. Take advantage of things that people before you did not have and don't hold yourself back, especially when you have an opportunity waiting for you. What is the worse that will happen? It will either go better or worse than your expectations. Even then, you will properly learn to manage your expectations and learn about your threshold to overwhelming situations. So, remember, to keep the flow going, you have to keep moving!

Rule #3

Never miss family time...

And never be the reason someone else does so either.

"Without the love and support of my mother, father, sisters, aunts, and uncles, I wouldn't have had the self-belief to strive to achieve."

Richard Branson

You now probably understand my admiration for Richard Branson and his values in life. Even scientifically, family support and loved ones have been shown to increase an individual's self-worth, and hence, the chances of a successful and happy life, and rightly so. I remember how my father used to focus on whatever little time we had together. Apart from working till evening most days, we would all sit together and have supper together where we would simply talk to each other about our day. My dad never spoke much but always made sure that we sat down and had some sort of interaction together, so every day, we all knew that we would have an eventful meal before we closed off the day.

The way I see it, family time is when you can disseminate all your negative energy out of your body by speaking to each other. Similarly, people often hang out with friends-like families for the same reason; to dismantle their most problematic and troublesome parts of the day.

I have mentioned this enough times already and will continue to do so no matter how anyone feels about it; we cannot replace the human touch! Humans need other human beings, and that is how we are just wired. And the best way to keep in touch with your most raw, human form is to mollycoddle with your family moments and have them as frequently as possible. Familial bonds can make or break your self-esteem and sense of self.

There is barely anyone out there who knows you as well as your family does. In some cases, you may have friends that know you inside out as well. A good social environment is the most influential aspect in building a successful person. Many people and experts argue that a nurturing home and school environment together maintain the soundness of decision making and risk-taking abilities in an individual, both extremely important aids to a person of substance. A person with a healthy balance of skills and judgment is more likely to flexibly make it in a world that may sometimes seem linear.

Once again, your environment is going to set the tone for the rest of your life, and it is up to you to keep upgrading yourself to meet your own standards. Your education and upbringing by your parents mean nothing if you are going to procrastinate when the time comes to show who you are. You really do strike while the rod is hot, or it becomes rather a task to mold yourself in a situation that seems like it is headed nowhere.

Sunday church was all about being together as a family and spending time together outside of the busy hustle of life. We were all a family of singers, and we made every effort to show it, especially when we presented ourselves in God's arena. My aunt Polly could play the piano very well, and I am convinced she had a gift to read music and sing like a canary. We would all get together at church and form a small family choir and have the time of our lives. I miss that time we would spend together because that truly drove empathy and the want to have a family of my own one day someday in me.

Your family and your home will always be your first learning space, and what you take from here will always stay with you. Entrepreneurs like me and many others that I follow always have a big emphasis on spending time with family and friends. Your safe space must be a constant where you can go where things feel overwhelming, and that is something you can only achieve with people with who you share an intimate bond.

CHAPTER 4:

THE JOURNEY BEGINS

It was in 1984 when I decided to move to the US with my wife back then. I had gotten married the second time, and after the devastation my first divorce left me with, I thought to myself, *'This is perfect. I am starting over, and this is exactly what I needed in life.'* I was happy, and all I wanted was to move away from everything I had ever known to start anew. My wife, Linda, was pregnant with our first child, and we were both extremely excited about where we were going in life.

When I met Linda, I felt like I was on the seventh heaven. My life felt complete, and I knew she was the one for me. I wanted to spend my life with her, and I wanted to give her the best life that I could provide, and that is exactly why I wanted to move to the United States of America, The Land of Opportunity, and start all over again.

My second wife came from a well-settled background, and we had both met at the IBM plant in Scotland, where I worked. Both our mothers were from Scotland, but her father was in the American Air Force, based in Scotland, so she had dual nationality. Linda loved her life in Scotland, but she missed her life in the US a lot more. She worked at a car rental company as a manager, and that is when I first saw her. She was also the manager of a car rental company back home in Scotland and came to IBM to negotiate a contract for corporate rental rates for cars that were present in her inventory. After a few sessions of speaking to her and getting to know who Linda really is, I knew I wanted to marry her. Fast forward to a couple almost a year later, we finally got married. And then, a few months later, into our marriage, I found out I was going to be a dad. I was ecstatic at the news. Although I had had two kids from my first marriage, this time, it felt different. I could not contain my happiness when I found out about the baby, and that was one of the driving forces that compelled me to think about starting life over once again in a new country. With only about two thousand dollars in my pocket and the hope for a better life, I said goodbye to my family, and we headed off to start our careers and lives once again.

My first divorce left me with feelings of emptiness and inadequacy. The love and understanding my parents had in their marriage were sacred, and I tried everything to recreate that in my life, but boy! Was I wrong? It took me a while to understand how marriages and women, in particular, function, but I am glad it happened. In retrospect, I do understand why my marriages failed and what I could have done better.

Linda was excited, too. I clearly remember how many times she told me that she was happy when I told her about moving to the US. She was done with

Scotland because of the bad weather. One day, I even remember that she came up to me and gave me an ultimatum just when she was a few months into her pregnancy.

"Brian, I can't live like this anymore. I am moving to America whether you like it or not. Please come with me if you can, but even if you cannot, I am still leaving," she said to me, leaving me astonished for a few seconds.

"Okay, Linda," I told her gently. "I hear you. I want to support you, so what I can do is take a sabbatical from my job, and we can go check out what life in America is like." Just then, I thought to myself, *'If it doesn't work out, I am coming right back to my old life.'*

We packed a few suitcases and began our journey. I would not say I was exactly worried, but I did have the thought of starting over once again in my mind, though. I knew I was going to find a way. I trusted my gut and took the next big step in my life, not knowing that the next few hours would be stressful until we actually stepped foot in the new country. Linda was sick through our flight. She had motion sickness that came with the early stages of pregnancy, and even after we got off the plane, we had to wait for quite a while before we would get a hold of our luggage which made me really anxious the whole time. I felt I was a little helpless at this point and thought, *'This is not a good omen at all.'*

When we first started settling in, I needed some help, so I contacted an IBM colleague who had previously lived in the States for an assignment but was currently in London – *what did I tell you about maintaining a good network?* We took a cab from the airport to his apartment, found his keys under the doormat, and stayed there for about eight weeks. I slowly started realizing that I could live here with my current job, so I reached out to the company, only to have them tell me that they were not transferring any employees at that time. I felt stuck again but proceeded to write them an application as they had instructed me to.

If there was anything I had learned from living in the past thirty years at that point in time was to keep living, you had to keep moving, and that is what I precisely did. I started looking for other opportunities to sustain myself and my wife.

I started looking for all kinds of jobs to get on my feet. I knew I could climb the stairs up and do something to sustain myself, but I had to work hard. I applied for truck driver positions and other such tertiary jobs, and I felt no shame doing so. My wife had gotten a job as a hotel receptionist before me, which gave me some contentment. We used my friend's car to get around. I would drive my wife to work and then utilize the vehicle for my job hunt. But soon enough, I realized that we would be needing our own cars and had a plan in mind. I heard an opening for a job in Mobile, Alabama, and instantly applied for it. I heard back from them, and on New Year's Eve, they invited me to join them at a fine-dining spot at the Peach Tree Plaza Hotel Bar. The meeting involved the founder of the company, who had a Scottish last name, and we instantly clicked. We spoke about our experiences in life so far, and once we started mingling, he even offered to fly me down to the city of Mobile, where the job was offered. I had been to the US multiple times when working for IBM, but this was the first time that I was going to be in Alabama. I was offered the job once I met the base team in the city and was to start in a week. Once I had secured my source of income, it was time to take care of the car problem.

This is where I would say my pure people skills came into play. I walked into a Ford dealership and met with the salesperson sitting behind his desk on a regular day – or so he thought. I walked up to him and told him the truth straight up. I introduced myself and told him my situation.

"I have no cash, no credit cards, and no bank account," I started. "I need two cars. One for me and one for my wife. We are new in the country, and we really need your help." And that day, I walked out of that dealership with two cars, only God knows how. I took a long shot but had I never asked, I would have never known what I was capable of. This act caused a new sense of confidence in me, and I was headed home with both the cars to give my wife the good news.... Or so I thought. We set off on the journey to Mobile but were separated in traffic.

It had been two days that my wife had not shown up. I had no way to contact her. After two nights of waiting, I decided to stay at home because I knew that my wife was a smart woman, and she would turn up at the apartment at least. I waited impatiently, worrying about how she must be feeling and if she had eaten something. A Baptist preacher had found her on the roadside because her car had run out of gas, and Linda was apparently in tears. I felt very poorly because I wanted to do more in that situation, but I really did the best I could by being home so I would be right here when she got back. The preacher told me that he had taken Linda home with him and his wife, and made sure they cared for her till she felt a little better to drive. I was grateful for his kindness and thanked him multiple times. I was just glad that Linda was all right. I spent the next few days taking care of her.

Richard Branson, too, talks about the importance of love in one's life. Many people know him for his excellent entrepreneurial skills, but not many people know that he has been in a committed relationship for about forty years now! I marvel at the bond that he has with his wife—a fulfilling relationship with a partner. As per my experience, it is much more wholesome than a full bank account or even a rich lifestyle because the comfort a companion gives you is like no other. In the words of Branson himself, he considers his loving relationship with his wife one of his biggest successes in life. Imagine that; a global multi-billionaire counting his blessings in the midst of a world that wants more and more. It really makes you wonder what the most important things in life are.

He once said in an interview that when he was younger, he thought love was an overwhelming feeling that made people fall head-over-heels for someone and make the heart sing, but then he proceeded to blame it on his pubescent self. However, the reality for him was far different from him. He was not in love with his wife, Joan, at first sight, much like in those Rom-Com movies and novels. In fact, he claims that he fell in love because of Joan's persistence and characteristics and not out of romance. It was the courage she brought out in him for being fearless and encouraging him to take risks while supporting him through all his fears and shortcomings. He also highlighted that a loving relationship is not all about sending each other love letters but the constant effort put in on a daily basis to make things work. Branson describes his forty-year-old relationship as a source of comfort and strength for him, his safe space. In his own words;

"Love should be supportive; it should lift us and inspire us to be the best possible person we can be. Because if you can be the best version of yourself, your partner will benefit too. That's the cornerstone of a great relationship – wanting the best for and bringing out the best in each other."

Although I learned this lesson quite a while later in my life, I am glad that I was able to learn it at all. We often expect marriage to be a box full of happiness and blessings. In reality, all we get is an empty box as soon as the officiator says, *'You may kiss the bride.'* From then on, it is up to the two people who have just finished saying out loud their vibes to each other to put consistent work into the relationship to make it work. You will achieve success in the direction that you put work in. Your best bet is balancing your personal and professional life because if you don't strike a balance, everything will come spiraling down.

Today's world is moving fast, and young people have little to no time to work on their relationships. All the generation today is required to do is keep at it at their desk jobs while missing out on life. I feel really sorry for bosses who treat their employees like robots, monitoring their every move, keeping them confined within their boxes. I have experienced firsthand the disastrous effect this has on people in the firm and the synergy between the teams, and it is not something to be proud of. If you are not making someone's life better on this planet, then you are wasting your time. And frankly, too many of us are not giving back to the community enough, drying up the resources we use.

I was just twenty-one years old when I first got married back in Greenock. Her name was Patricia, and when I look back at that marriage, I think I rushed into it. After I got married, I was working for IBM, and I had the opportunity to travel all over the world. Every time I would go to a new place, I would think about how much I was missing out on. The world has fascinated me. I feel like it is so much you can see and explore, not just about the Earth we live in but also about ourselves. I learned so much about myself when I was traveling on my own.

Regardless, Patricia and I had a strong bond that I miss to this day. We were not just a couple, but we are also very good friends. The divorce was hard on me, but I cannot even imagine what she went through to readjust to life after two kids. I still got to go to work and focus on my career, but Patricia, as a mother, had her whole life turned upside down. At times, I feel misled and think that she might have, too.

Everything I went through, the lows, negatives, and hopelessness, all bottled up inside me as I always thought that is the way you deal with feelings. I never opened them up again, but they did leave a detrimental effect on me. Every time I ended a relationship, these feelings kept getting cooped up inside me till they were too much for me to handle. My coping mechanism was to drown myself in work, and, to be honest, it worked because I would always focus my energy more and more on getting better. Of course, I realized later that working on another aspect in life is not a way to move on from a different sort of pain. My personal problems were not going to shrink if my success got bigger. I have seven biological children, out of which two are daughters, and five are sons. And two inherited dependents out of one of my marriages which I took the responsibility of.

I had two children out of my first marriage, namely Niven and Pauline. They were both born in Scotland, and after my wife and I got separated, she won sole custody of them, and even when I left the country, Patricia took complete care of them.

I have to give it to Patricia for pulling through on her own even after twelve years of marriage. It ideally takes about sixty days to build a habit, and to live with someone for that long makes people dependent on each other. I still consider Patricia a good friend of mine as she was and still is a wonderful person. It is unfortunate that we drifted apart because we made a good, functional couple, but we did not do very well as married partners.

My second marriage ended for similar reasons. Linda gave me two beautiful children named Adrian and Victoria. This time, unlike my first marriage, I tried my best to keep my older son with me as the younger one was too young to live without her mother, and I finally succeeded. My wife even tried to convince me that the child was not mine which broke my heart, but I still went ahead and fought for my children. I knew I had to do something, and I did not stop at anything to keep him.

My relationship with Linda only lasted about five years. To make things worse, I also found out that she was having an affair with another man behind my back. Supposedly, the same man whose baby she convinced me she was carrying. I was traveling to California and was in Las Vegas when I came to find that I was being cheated on. I did know what to say.

I did not realize this back then and would ask myself the same question, thinking, *'Why does this happen to me?'* But years later, I understood why my marriages would always end. Linda would ask me for time and attention in many different ways, but I have always been a workaholic. I always wanted to grow and excel at my career, forgetting that my personal life is also equally important. It is not uncommon to focus your energy in one direction, from the way I see it. Hence, anyone I speak to, I focus on the importance of balance in life.

Soon after I left my second wife, I took my older son Adrian and moved to Los Gatos, California, where I thought I would start my life over. You know, when I was younger, I did not have many privileges, but when I had kids, I made sure that this would never happen to them. Coming out of high school, I was once listening to The Beatles – which is not common because I did not really listen to much music owing to the fact that we never owned a radio or a TV at home.

'When I am older,' I thought to myself, *'I will ensure my kids always have what they want.'*

I decided to go to California with Adrian. Once I made up my mind and got a go-ahead from my lawyers, I packed my bags, gathered my golf clubs, my clothes, and all of my booze to go across the country. I made sure I had everything, especially things little Adrian would need on our way till we at least made it to California, where we were headed. When we got there, I rented an apartment and made advanced payments for up to six months so I would not have to worry about things instantly. After settling, I knew I had to do something for Adrian while I would go away to work every day. I could not afford daycare at that point, and I also needed someone I could trust. I thought about a colleague of mine who lived in Germany and whose relatives were looking forward to working in the US. In an instant, I picked up the phone and called him up, asking him if he had any kids, nephews, or nieces who would like to work in California for the next six months while helping me take care of Adrian. I thought about how this two-way relationship could be fruitful in the sense that if we both contribute some portion of our day to raise Adrian, both of us could focus on our career and soon when Adrian is old enough to do some basic tasks on his own and start schooling, I would come up with a different routine for him so things can be easier.

My colleague understood my situation. Luckily enough, his niece, Christine, was looking for work outside of the country, and he told me that she could join me and help me raise Adrian. Once a week to once a month, I used to go to Las Vegas to sow my wild roots as a way to get away from life when it got heavy. Something I really needed to stay grounded while competing in the race of life. I would often go to Las Vegas after a few months of settling into the place, and that is when I met my third wife. When I first saw her, I thought I recognized her from somewhere, but I could not quite put my finger on it. And then it finally clicked! She was my colleague from Mobile,

Alabama. We had no romantic connection or attraction between us at first. We would just talk and get to know each other the first few times that we met. But soon after, she came to me and told me that she had gotten pregnant with my child. I was shocked, and I did not know what to do. We had a drunken, crazy night, and things had gotten way out of hand, but it was too late to look back now. She told me that she wanted to terminate the pregnancy and was adamant about it. I understood where she was coming from, but the act of abortion would go against my most basic belief system and, hence, I strongly stood against it. I would not let a baby, a human being, get killed just because we adults had made a mistake. In fact, this was all the more reason that we had to step up and take action. And the bottom line of that relationship was;

> "What happens in Vegas cannot always stay
> in Vegas."

It is the truth because it was not just a fling or even a full-blown affair that we could just sweep under the rug. We had a baby on the way, and there was no way in hell I was letting this child have a bad life or be a bad father once again. It was once again time for me to step up and be the father I knew I was capable of. When we got back to Alabama, we instantly got married. My then-wife was seven months pregnant, and we got married at Carmel by the sea. It was a beautiful, scenic wedding that I very much enjoyed. My third marriage started out of an impulsive decision one crazy night and stayed that way just like that, I was now officially the father of five kids, two from two marriages, and one from my third.

However, by the time my younger child was three, my marriage was already in tatters, and shortly after that, I had gotten divorced for the third time in my life. I was frustrated, and I did not know what to do. I felt broken and alone once again, trying to find out what went wrong. But in my heart, I knew that this marriage should not have happened in the first place because it started off under the wrong circumstances.

Once again, I doused myself in work because it was the only thing that I knew. My entire life felt like it was falling apart and, because I was good at what I did, even back then, I started working again. I worked hard and helped build a company. I grew this company considerably, taking care of operations and making sure that we made a healthy number of sales. After the company was flourishing, I sold it to another company for a good price in San Diego. Shortly after, I moved to San Diego with my young son and started consulting for another company that was looking for expert opinions, recommendations, and analysis for its company-wide operations. I was good at it and worked as hard as I could to get everything else off my mind. Eventually, I became the CEO and ultimately the chairman of the board for that company. I have been in San Diego since then. I worked with the same company for a while and honed my skills even more. I really enjoyed what I did and still do to this day. I was about fifty years old back then, and I was content with what I was doing... And that is when I found my fourth wife.

She was a beautiful woman, definitely an ego boost for me because I had married a good-looking, much younger woman. I had two more sons out of my marriage with her. Life was good. I was finally beginning to believe that she was the one for me and that we would live happily ever after. My fourth marriage lasted for about twelve years, but, unfortunately, like all my other marriages up to that point, it came with an expiration date, too. I found out she was cheating on me with her personal trainer, and this time, I was furious. I fought, once again, for the custody of my two sons. I figured the personal trainer did not have much to offer anyway, so I had a fair chance to win my children anyway.

The custody of any of my children was never a messy one, and I intended to keep it that way. In my opinion, the stupidest thing parents can do is fight and quarrel in front of their young children. I wanted my kids to love both their parents, regardless of what happened with my wives. This time around, I bought a house not too far away for my ex-wife so my children could visit both of us regularly. I built a reasonable relationship with all my ex-wives on behalf of my children.

There will come the point in your life when you begin to plodder. At this point, everything feels like a mess because you feel you are not getting where you want, although everything else is working fine. Sometimes, you will become short-sighted because you will feel fixated at one specific point, and it will feel like you are stuck in a rut, or rather a cycle, where you are chasing your own tail. The effort you put into relationships, personal or professional, will come with a hint of doubt behind them, while the energy you exert into your surroundings starts to dull down. I am here to tell you that everyone reaches this point in life, and it is normal to feel low and hopeless when things begin to feel stuck in their ways. It is human nature to get fed up when things do not go their way.

However, the good news is that it is not the end of everything. You see, life comes and goes in waves. One year you will feel at your highest point, and maybe the next, you will begin to think that things have absolutely gone into the crapper. But it is not true. That is not how life works. It does not work according to your expectations. So, the silver lining is that when you expect that life will always be murky and negative, the chances are that acceleration is right around the corner, hopefully in the form of good news.

I had nearly given up all hope when my fourth marriage ended. I was in the exact situation as I have described. My mind was already convincing me to change my outlook on love and relationships, to accept that love is not for everyone, and simply move on with dating and casual relationships. I mean, I could just live with an open mind and let go of the nasty breakups and split-ups, sparing myself the heartache.

I remember this one time when I had freshly gotten back home from the hospital with a lung disease when one of my wives had told me they were leaving me. I was on bed rest, attached to an oxygen machine, with a thirty-foot tube connected between me so my breathing would not be compromised. I watched my wife enter the house, scrambling through and taking away the things we had gotten together. I did not have the energy to move, and I certainly did not know what to say to her. I just watched in silence as she moved around, going through things and gathering what she found interesting. There was an overwhelming, disturbing vibe inside the house, and I could not shake the negative, leftover feelings that took over me. I just watched in silence till she finally spoke to me.

"I am taking the things that belong to me," she finally spoke to me after she had been around the house at least twice and still counting. I did not know what to say to her, but this maneuver made me angry. I looked into her eyes for a few seconds before I spoke.

"I don't need the things. Take what you want and just leave. I can start over," is what I could finally muster. I went into my room and closed the door behind me, and that is when I saw her for the last time. That's what I did. Once I was better in terms of my health, I slowly started getting back to my life. The negative feelings started to wash off as I excelled at work once again. I felt my confidence coming back, and that is when I decided how stupid fighting in a divorce is. I realized the amount of money I had spent, and I was still not happy after separating. The only people who benefit from such settlements and situations are the ruthless lawyers who fight our cases. I wanted to be civil through the process for the sake of my children, and that is what I did. I let my wife have what she wanted, and I focused on rebuilding myself and still kept climbing the career ladder.

I was about sixty-two or sixty-three years old when I thought I had had enough of relationships and romance. I was convinced that the marriage game is not for me, and given my past experiences, you would agree, too. I was mentally not ready to get into the dating game, but before that, I was making my mind up about getting an au pair for my children. I thought that this au pair would take care of my dependents, and on days that my kids were visiting their mothers, the au pair would just take care of me. I had also thought I would change this caretaker every six months. I had booked a flight to the Czech Republic to bring back this au pair with me, but life had something else planned for me at this point.

My seventy-four years have taught me an important lesson. I like to think that life is like riding a bicycle. When you start to get on the bicycle, you do not get too far. It takes you a while to get a smooth grip and a somewhat level ride. As you grow up, the road gets tougher, and you need to practice your grip even more. When you fall on rocky terrain, you get up, dust yourself off, and climb back up. You ride it again, and along the way, you also help your friends and family and vice versa. When you become a pro at riding the bike and anticipating the situation of the road ahead, you hang in there, facing the storm with strong-headedness. I personally think that is where I am in life. I have finally learned to maneuver my way through a relationship after being in so many. But I did not get here without my fair share of ups and downs. In fact, the more prepared I thought I was with every proceeding step, I came to realize the tougher the road got, but I kept holding onto my handlebars and clutched the brake when the situation got too overwhelming. I did not get there all alone, don't get me wrong. I had my family and friends to get me along the way, and I am very grateful for how far I have come.

CHAPTER 5:

THE BIGGEST TEACHER

When we think about the terms 'loss' or 'grief,' we crudely think about the tug of war between life and death. The connotation around such terms has been assigned to a certain level of morbidity when the truth is much further from reality. Terms that have to do with losing someone or something in life are much broader, and their perception and comprehension as per our understanding can change our view of life. It is safe to say that there is no one in the world who does not go through loss and forfeiture. If someone says they have never lost something, they are living a lie that will catch up to them when it is least expected. It is inevitable for us humans to gain and lose even parts of ourselves as we grow up and go through different phases in life.

Grief will teach you many lessons, and the biggest one will be that nearly everything you come across is temporary; the money you are chasing, the big house you are planning on building, and the car you are working so hard to keep spotless. The only thing that will speak your story is your legacy and what you did to make it. Have you ever heard someone say, *'Joshua was a rich guy. He had the biggest house in the neighborhood,'* to remember the deceased at a funeral? The only things people will remember are the presence you had in their life, the impact you caused, but, more importantly, the way you made them feel. We, ourselves, forget what we intangibly did for the people around us, but we never forget the feelings we had for them that led us to do something quantifiable for them. Once again, what humans can do for each other cannot be replaced by intangible wealth and material affluence, or worldly treasures. I know people who know each other based on the first time they met each other, myself included. The pandemic that hit the world earlier last year has put many things into perspective, including the fact that life on earth is fragile. Many millionaires and billionaires lost their lives to a simple micro virus despite having the entire world at their feet. Ask yourself what their wealth did for them, and then assess for yourself how important money really is and how much importance you should be attaching to it.

The nature of grief or loss each person goes through is just as unique as the individual him or herself. Even when two individuals go through the same unfortunate fate, their experiences will be different because so is their specific understanding of the event. If one person is more sensitive and receptive to traumatic loss events, does this mean that the less sensitized person's loss is less in magnitude? Of course, not! This is why quantifying grief, loss, pain, and agony is not possible because calculating the individual facets of one's life is simply not possible.

We came into this world without any timetables or linear progression charts to justify or rationalize our pain or its threshold. Some people recover from discomfort resulting from hurtful events in a few days, while for others, one event can be life-changing. Sometimes, the recovery process is so heavy that there are multiple setbacks and moments of hopelessness along the way. Can you relate?

We all know the five stages of grief; *denial, anger, bargaining, depression, and acceptance.* Every person takes a different route and journey through these stages as well. Grief is just as picky when it comes to different people as people are when it comes to things that make them happy.

Grief that follows loss is difficult to trace because there are no set symptoms that even a professional can instantly point out. Often, therapists and psychologists have to work with their patients before prescribing a certain treatment method and medication to help them. However, there are some common signs that people exhibit subconsciously that can help identify the problem and then track down its effect on the person.

• **Sadness**

Now, sadness does not always manifest itself as a frown on someone's face. When someone is sad, they often opt for isolation and take a liking to be by themselves, preferring loneliness and alone time over conversing about what they are feeling. Humans suffering from sadness also often believe that their pain is not understandable, which drives them further down into their spiral of sorrow and despair.

• Shock/disbelief

When you receive news that comes as a shock, your brain actively works to refuse it, shutting itself down to protect you from shock and surprise. People have often reported becoming numb after losing a close one or receiving shocking news – this ordeal is not unusual. Individuals exhibit a reluctance and unwilling attitude when they hear about the loss. Even entrepreneurs have coping mechanisms if a monetary or financial loss occurs during their important transactions.

• Anger

Whether you understand it or not, anger is an emotion that will almost always linger around to manifest itself when a situation seems overwhelming. But what no one tells you is that anger is usually a symptom of an underlying feeling such as hurt or betrayal. It is common to think, *'Life is unfair,'* or *'God is responsible for this,'* when one does not understand or cannot justify a loss that has occurred. This void grows so deep over time that even the smallest inconvenience seems like a big deal, disrupting your attitude and reshaping your behavior if carried inside over a period of time.

- **Fear**

  When you lose someone or something you depend on, you instantly begin to think you will be lost without their presence or support forever. Facing life without your rock seems impossible, and your mind starts feeding you all kinds of thoughts, convincing you that life is difficult now and things will never be the same again.

- **Guilt**

  Loss in life will have you fretting over the littlest things you said or the things you did not do while you had the chance. But I am here to tell you that there is possibly nothing you could have done to change the outcome. Of course, you must try to maintain positive, healthy relationships and attachments and nurture people with your positivity and optimism, but grief and loss are set in stone. You can do absolutely nothing to avoid either.

It does not stop there. The ebb and flow of life bring many other such events, of not with you than with others, that will trigger 'secondhand grief' inside of you. When you hear about someone else's loss, you will experience your situation in the past again. Or, if you were young when you experienced a painful event, you might have gone through some developmental issues that have made you vulnerable to the news of grief or loss. Every time you hear of someone's loss, you can't help but at least think about the last time you went through a detrimental loss.

Like nearly all problems in life, overcoming grief or loss require that you acknowledge and accept that you are affected first. Everyone goes through feelings of grief and loss, but the aim is to process these situations onset, so they do not leave a burning void inside of you, rendering you hollow and paralyzing you on a daily basis. The following poem about loss always gives me hope to keep moving.

Before you know what kindness really is
you must lose things,
feel the future dissolve in a moment
Like salt in a weakened broth.
What you held in your hand,
what you counted and carefully saved,
all this must go so you know
how desolate the landscape can be
Between the regions of kindness.

How you ride and ride
thinking the bus will never stop,
the passengers eating maize and chicken
Will stare out the window forever.

Before you learn the tender gravity of kindness
you must travel where the Indian in a white poncho
Lies dead by the side of the road.
You must see how this could be you,
how he too was someone
who journeyed through the night with plans
And the simple breath that kept him alive.

Before you know kindness as the deepest thing inside,
You must know sorrow as the other deepest thing.
You must wake up with sorrow.
You must speak to it till your voice
catches the thread of all sorrows
And you see the size of the cloth.
Then it is only kindness that makes sense anymore,
only kindness that ties your shoes
and sends you out into the day to gaze at bread,
only kindness that raises its head
from the crowd of the world to say
It is I you have been looking for,
and then goes with you everywhere
Like a shadow or a friend.

~

Kindness, Naomi Shihab Nye - 1952

Every time one of my wives left me, I went into my beat mode, where I would work to the bone. To make up for losses and recalcitrance in my life, I took further control of what I knew and took pride in the fact that there was and still is one aspect in my life that I could control. A part of me does acknowledge that I rushed into relationships just for the sake of companionship, but I did what I thought was best at the time, and if anything, I am a better man for learning from it. When things started slipping, I initially would look for different routes to exert my energy. For instance, I would contest for the custody of my kids, leave town, try to figure things that I knew would result in success because I could never wrap my head around the fact that the situation was out of my control.

The way I see it, life repeated the same lesson again and again till I took away the learning from it that was meant for me. Had I always been the same Brian who worked day and night, trying to reach his goals, I would never be able to be the family man I wanted to be. The universe works in mysterious ways, and while there are only a few times you might understand what it is trying to tell you, I can assure you that it gives you countless signs of what lies ahead. It is only a matter of being able to receive and understand what is being told to you. And for this comprehension, it is absolutely necessary that you stay clear in your head. To do so, you need to resolve your underlying emotions, so your judgment is not clouded.

During difficult times, it is important to realize that life does not owe you anything, and everything that happens is for a reason. Once you realize that everything here has a fixed time on Earth, you will slowly start to understand how things work. Once again, easier said than done, but the more you convince yourself of this reality, the easier it will be for you to get through life. Losing my Daddy John, going through multiple divorces, having my parents leave due to old age, and facing the loss of my young sons would have rendered me useless and hopeless had I not opened myself up to the reality of the situation and accepted what had happened to me.

Lessons By Grief and Loss

One definite lesson I have learned through the ups and downs of life is that change is consistent. Be it in the profit and loss statement of a company you have started or the number of people in your life. You win some, you lose some, and that is the only thing life guarantees. Life takes you on different journeys that shape you as a person because of the lessons you take from it. For instance, I can either learn to move forward in the face of failure or reject failure altogether. Either way, that lesson will specifically be for me to learn. If I were to summarize a few key lessons I have learned after grieving the loss of loved ones and favorable situations, they would be as follows:

1. Some losses will always be grieved over. This statement is especially true for people who leave your life. People are precious and irreplaceable. When Daddy John left me, I was in tatters. I miss him every day and the wealth of knowledge he brought into my life, but the truth of the matter is that he is gone. All I remember of him now is his legacy, his entrepreneurial wisdom, acumen, and tips he transferred to me when I was growing up.

   My life completely changed after my sons were gone. I had two options post their deaths; to challenge my tragedy and reject reality or accept what had happened to them and acknowledge my loss so the grief process could begin. Easier said than done, but take it from someone who did it, I took my time to grief and chose to take a step forward. I am still grieving after all this time, but it is either not being able to function without them or remembering them through happy, healthy memories while honoring their death by doing what is right for them.

2. The life following a loss will teach you that carrying on while you are grieving is hard, but you have to do your best to create a new normal. By the time my fourth wife had left me, I was beginning to lose hope about ever being able

to find love and settling down. As a man who wanted a happy, healthy family, I soon began to see my self-image as a father and family man disappearing. I had convinced myself that I would just engage in casual dating for the rest of my life while the person who is intended to spend the rest of my life with me will walk into my life if ever and whenever she is meant to.

When I lost my parents, the feeling of heartbreak and disbelief was the same. Although I was not dependent on them, and I was traveling the world when I received the news both times, I can sometimes still feel the silence of their absence ringing in my ears louder than ever. And the worst part is that this grief never got old because I still think about them often, wondering what life would be like had they still been here with me.

3. Grief has taught me that life is fragile and that death is just one breath away. Read that again. Every breath that you take could be your last one. This makes me grateful for the life I have had, accepting what is sent my way, and being patient for the things that are taken away from me. The losses we face will always be a part of us, but what they make us feel is what will truly be the deciding factor of our failures or

successes. I learned from my father and my Daddy John to grab every opportunity that you can while it lasts and no task is too small or stupid to be done. I mean, Daddy John learned to chop chickens and sold them over Christmas to benefit from the occasion and opportunity.

4. Don't give yourself a timeline to grieve because there is no such thing. That's right. You are your own person, and you need to do you to get out of any situation that affects you. All these years, the collective loss of family has taught me that no matter how hard you try to rush the grieving and healing process, it will take its own time to wash over you. Then, finally, you will strengthen yourself enough to not let it affect you. The time it takes for you to not be able to get out of bed because of the heaviness of loss to the point that you smile thinking about all the times they made you happy is a voyage on its own. I try to remind myself that the loss equals the love I have for them. Slowly, as time passes by, you learn to live with it. Again, I am a firm believer that you do not really get over it, but you cope up to the point that the pain does not cripple you on an everyday basis. The part of themselves they gave to you, and vice versa, will permanently remain with you.

5. For the longest time, accepting the good that happened to me was difficult without immediately thinking about what I had lost in my life. Losing someone close to you puts you in a place of fear, where you might constantly have your guard up, thinking about when the next tragedy might strike. At least, that is what happened to me. After losing several people with who I was close, I began thinking everything comes with a fixed timeline and an expiration date. The devastating pain changed my perception of life, but my take on the good events in life helped me overcome this negative point of view. I learned that life was still going to happen to me and the only way to get by in life was to appreciate what I was given and accept that which has been taken away. There is no point in fighting your circumstances. Be humble and keep your head high so you can keep moving forward.

Moving Along with Grief

I will not tell you that you can move on from loss because the grief will sometimes follow you forever. It will hit you when you least expect it, and you might not even be aware when it happens. The most important thing to remember is to take care of yourself while your inner self grieves the loss that is occupying your energy. We often forget that even the negatives in our lives need to be nurtured till they no longer become detrimental to our health. Loss has the bad rep to suck out your energy, directly fluctuate your energy, and feed on your emotional reservoir, rendering you void of energy to focus on anything else. If you keep ignoring your emotional and mental needs, they will have a ripple effect that will slow you down in all other areas of life. Sure, your personal and professional lives are separate, but you need to understand that the engine – *you* – driving the two spaces is the same, and just as a good day at home boosts your productivity at work, negativity in your personal life will also follow you to your workplace. If what we have spoken on grief and loss makes sense to you so far, you will be willing to work out the confusing parts of life to get ahead. You may use the next few pages as a manual if you are looking to work on yourself and heal because the tips below have helped me, at least in real-time, to figure out the nitty-gritty details in my life.

Taking Care of Your Grieving Self

1. Go easy on yourself

This fact is something that seems impossible at times but is crucially important. We are so invested in the race of life to accumulate wealth and money that everything else seems secondary, especially self-care and taking a break. Taking your eyes off the prize seems like you might lose everything, and while it is not true at all, shutting the world out for a few minutes a day to focus on your surroundings helps you keep yourself grounded. The most underrated, quick reset button is the act of taking a deep breathe to drown out the noise around you. Breathe often and try to re-focus your energy to boost your motivation multiple times a day.

2. Tangibly express your energy

Practicing creativity and physical means of expression is something that has always helped me cope with loss. I would go ahead and help others around me to help me manage my feelings of negativity. I would try to remind myself that I had no agency around the workings of the universe, and we all have a specific duration. What this also helped me learn was that human connection is sacred and volatile. So, nurture your relationships while you can because everything on Earth is limited, your time here included.

3. Allow yourself to grieve

Feel what you have to so the residual feelings can be processed timely. Repressing your emotions is only another way of prolonging your suffering, which is not healthy for the human body. If left unprocessed, grief and hurt can have adverse physiological and emotional manifestations that lead to depression, anxiety, and other such problems.

4. Involve yourself in physical activity

Your body and mind are part of one whole unit, and hence, will always be connected. Exercising your physical health promotes emotional healing, discouraging mental lethargy and exhaustion that are common symptoms of grief followed by loss. On days when you do not understand what to do with the negativity inside you, going for a run or jog helps take the edge of the situation. Simple things such as getting ample sleep or having comfort foods will make you feel stable and keep you sane.

CHAPTER 6:

A HUMAN AFTERALL

"The one who falls and gets up is stronger than the one who never tried. Do not fear failure but rather fear not trying."

Paulo Coelho

The word 'failure' has a downright negative connotation to it. People think failing at something is a setback that must be hidden from the world. Often, when children are younger and fail at school, their parents themselves hide the truth from other parents and family to save themselves and their kid from the 'shame' and 'embarrassment that follows. Although this humiliation often just exists in their head.

Dreading failure is so far embedded in our heads that we often give up things that seem too difficult, too impractical, or too different just because we attach a perception in our head regarding how the result may turn out. Although we, ourselves, are unaware of the results, we just try too hard to control things. From an F on our exams and tests to Failure in a new business venture, we think we have it all figured out. But, is it so?

According to Psychology Today, when people think of failure, they automatically have a far-sighted vision of the result. The fear of failure has an effect on your perception of the goals you set your heart on, killing them way before you even work on them. Failure has the power to distort your ambitions, keeping you mediocre and close to the things you already know. People often forget to step out of their heads and look at things from a fresh perspective. While this is not easy, you have to remember that this starts with *you*. As long as you keep thinking, 'I can't do this because xyz,' you will not be able to do it even if it is right in front of you. The 'what ifs' and 'could haves' are the most common terminologies you will hear out of the mouth of quitters and those that simply did not choose to look beyond the possibility of failure before they even got started.

Failure will also sow a seed of insecurity and doubt in your head regarding your own capabilities. How so? Once you start thinking of all the ways something could go wrong, you evaluate your intelligence, skills, and abilities through a broken lens that misrepresents your true competence. You will view yourself weaker, less smart than those around you, and even less important to be working on something that seems 'too out there.' As sad as it is, the fear behind disappointment and failure is a monster that exists only in your head.

When you fall down and find yourself not where you wanted to be, you take it very personally.

It is common for one to begin thinking that the failure was explicitly meant for them and that they will never be able to get out of it, especially at the very moment. However, setbacks and defeat have no personal agenda. My failure in relationships did not scream, 'I have to get Brian Bonar, so he feels poorly about himself.' When you take it personally, failure will create a deep, emotional wound that will have you on your knees for a long time. You will feel helpless and abandoned, fighting all by yourself merely because you think no one understands your struggle in life. Such feelings are not uncommon but fostering them bears the worst outcome where one starts thinking that success is just not meant for them. Falling into this void is like starting into quicksand and slipping into a bottomless pit that will likely rob one of future success. But when you are at your lowest, your mind will play the dirtiest tricks on you to keep you there.

Feelings of self-sabotage are inevitable when you think of someone who sits himself down after one or some failed experiments. Most times, you do not even realize the fear failure is causing inside you, which is the furthest from reality. When you do not address this sinking feeling of disappointment every time you think of doing something new, it is highly likely that you will stay one step behind no matter where you get in life. This subconscious conditioning reduces the likelihood of envisioning success, causing the individual to act emotionally instead of using reason to assess the situation.

Speaking of conditioning, many times, the irrational fear that our parents carry with themselves comes from their parents, which they, in turn, are put into us. It is common for parents to subconsciously or consciously punish their children when they go through small failures as they grow up. Emotionally withdrawing oneself, reacting in a harsh manner, and sometimes even getting verbally turbulent are all common practices by parents that instill an onset fear of failure in children. This behavior towards kids makes them feel like they are not good enough, and if parents continue being dismissive and ignorant, children grow up to feel inadequate nearly all their lives. A lack of self-appreciation often leaves children to work themselves to the bone in order to avoid failure and feelings of insufficiency in the future.

Repressing such feelings and constantly criticizing oneself leads to physical eruptions of emotional turmoil on the inside, resulting in anxiety, which leads to choking. The choking mechanism comes into play when anxiety makes you overthink something the brain already knows how to do. As a result, your body feels thrown off as the brain sends confusing signals to your motor body system, and you screw up the littlest of things. In essence, overthinking and burdening yourself leads to negative physical incapacitating such as choking, et cetera.

Although 'willpower' seems like an intangible concept, sprouting from within, it really depends on how active your body is for it to work. When you are fatigued, and your body is running on adrenaline, your willpower will not work. In fact, it will fail you. But it is not your body's fault that it is tired. Your inability to know when to stop is. Your capacity to compensate your body for overthinking and reimburse improper nourishment levels is what is going to keep you going. Maintaining glucose levels in your brain is essential for your cognitive function, executive roles, and willpower. If your ability to think and comprehend, plan and make decisions, and the determination respectively. Putting this fact into perspective, you will understand why studying only a few days before the exam, or even fad diets for that matter, end up disastrously, with the person often failing to achieve the purpose they had in mind.

Once you start spinning out of control, it is easy for your mind to get the best of you. You are as much your enemy as you are your own friend. Psychologists Amos Tversky and Daniel Kahneman found that the loss resulting from failure is twice as much as the gain from a victory. It is no wonder that people will go to great extents to avoid failure.

Talking About Your Failures

Human beings naturally share their achievements while they hide their failure as they would a big mole on their face. Failure is seen to erode confidence, making people feel like a public embarrassment. Feeling lowered in the eyes of others is an emotion anyone would try to avoid, like the plague. However, people need to know that talking about their failures – not parading them – can offer a wealth of experience to those around them. If disseminated properly, the society as a whole can gain knowledge through the experience of others.

When one goes through a failed situation, the first line of action should be to feel the loss. Are you feeling angry? Sad? Guilty? Or ashamed? Whatever it is, think about your feelings and reflect upon them. Feeling embarrassed would not be an option if you had given your best efforts. Look at it this way. If there are ten ways of doing something and you have failed at it twice, you are eight steps closer to your goal, and now you know what works and what does not! Acknowledgment of what you feel is first important to move to the next step.

You also have to accept a certain level of responsibility to own up to your failure. Immediately trying to ditch the situation to avoid accusations is no way to move ahead from your situation. Additionally, putting the blame on others is also not an option merely because it is not going to solve the problem. On the contrary, once all parties have accepted their flaws and responsibilities, it is easier to pinpoint the gaps in the situation. There is no excuse to back out, and you, of all people, should be figuring out other ways of moving forward than letting setbacks get the best of you.

Throughout history, all big inventions and inventions are backed by the evidence that minute issues can act as a hurdle in certain situations. The Wright brothers, for instance, tried for several years before their first aeroplane took off. They failed many times, just like Guglielmo Marconi and Thomas Alva Edison before they made their way to the newspaper headlines all over the world!

Of course, their struggles also started small. Many of them we may never know, but something we can get behind is the fact that they all had perseverance in common. Successful people have the quality of critical self-reflection that keeps them close to their goal with laser focus. As long as you know what you are doing and keep at it, you will get there.

Before you even start, the most important task is that you have everything in blueprint. I am not a big fan of planning and creating multiple to-do lists, but there should be a degree of homework that will provide you with the direction to follow through with your tasks.

On your journey, you will come across many instances when you will want to give up. You may observe your surroundings and see people who are much more relaxed, taking it slow, and even enjoying their lives without putting in much work but all you need to do is keep your eyes on the prize.

Success is so glamorized that anything else but coming out the other side shining, covered in glitter, is considered a failure. While nobody has the Midas Touch, the whole world thinks entrepreneurs and successful people do. Overnight tycoons and business professionals are not a thing, no matter how society sees them. Every bit of success is backed by sheer hard work and dedication. From my personal experience, I can confidently say that there is no man who has not experienced a failure that shook him to the core. Or a woman who had second thoughts after things went the way she did not plan in life. But as I have already mentioned, there is not a single successful person who paved their own way without crossing mountains and swimming through oceans.

Most people think about famous Hollywood celebrities and men in suits working as stockbrokers when they think 'success.' And while that image is not wrong, it is only a small percentage of people in a limited number of industries who look like that.

Failure and Expert Opinion

Richard Branson started his first charity when he was only seventeen. As he grew up and evolved within his role while working for Virgin, he started multiple verticals that did not work out for too long. We all know where and how Richard began his career, but that did not stop him from working as hard as he could to make his way up the ladder. His story also teaches us that success is a friend to no one. Be it a man born with a silver spoon in his mouth or one who has had to work from scratch to build his life, we all have to work to secure our place on earth just like our ancestors probably did according to their time and era.

When most tweens are enjoying their lives, hanging out with friends, and understanding the purpose of their lives, Richard Branson started the Virgin brand when he was about twenty years of age in 1970. His company's motto is 'Screw it, let's do it,' and it reflects his exact attitude through life. It makes sense if you think about it because, in the past several years since the launch of the brand, he has innovated and initiated many business ideas. There are currently about sixty Virgin companies under the same brand in thirty-five countries.

'We have never been 100% sure that any of the businesses we've started at Virgin were going to be successful,' he said at an interview. He also openly

talks about his failed businesses, never hiding them, assuming that failure will bring embarrassment. In fact, he openly wears his efforts as a badge of honor, discussing what went wrong. His approach has always been to focus on the silver linings, especially those that help people, and himself, benefit from the teachings. According to Richard in multiple interviews, only planning and strategizing is not enough unless you jump right into the idea because the right moment is always made.

In 1994, Richard Branson and the Virgin group launched Virgin Cola. The brand was increasingly growing in popularity, especially back then, since the launch of Virgin Atlantic Airlines, which was marketed vastly, but shortly after its first, disastrous test flight took off, the business had some trouble as well. The Virgin logo was also gaining some recognition and its association with local trains, video games, and radio stations. The brand was also expanding into mobile devices, the healthcare industry, and so much more.

According to his insight, Richard Branson saw an opportunity in the cola-flavored soda industry and his feasibility reports bolstered his confidence to take the idea forward. With a price point similar to its competitors, decent marketing, and ease to manufacture, Virgin Cola entered the market. However, the big market sharks got to him as soon as he started and leveraged their experience, market share, and influence on the mass to outlast the new entrant. As a result, Coca-Cola and Pepsi coalesced, while Coca-Cola increased its marketing budget, pressuring distributors to give up on distributing Virgin Cola.

'Declaring a soft drink war on Coke was madness,' said Branson in an interview post pulling the brand out of the market. *'I consider our cola venture to be one of the biggest mistakes we ever made – but I still wouldn't change a thing.'*

Then again, in 1996, Richard Branson launched his bridal boutique and wedding dress brand, named Virgin Brides. This chain of stores was inaugurated throughout multiple locations in London, where Branson got clean-shaven and put on a dress himself to market for the brand himself. Compared to other businesses, this venture lasted much longer till 2007. Branson tried to expand further into the fashion industry, launching an underwear label to compete with the famous competitor Victoria's Secret, but it, too, crashed and burned as the market was too established for the Virgin brand to proceed forward.

Shortly after, Branson introduced V2 Records that performed very well in the world record industry. He still decided to focus on the airline business, launching other affordable options in the European and American markets such as Virgin Express, Virgin

Blue, and Virgin American in Australia and the United States. The Virgin Group also launched a global Virgin Megastore chain that was a mix between a bookstore, a music store and also contained gadgets, et cetera. Speaking of gadgets – and this should not come as a surprise – Branson also launched Virgin Net and Virgin Mobile and entered the telecommunication industry in 1998. These ventures were a huge success for him.

In 2000, Virgin Cars were introduced into the market, where the purpose of the brand was to change the way cars were being traded in the industry. However, the company did not do too well, but the bright side of this venture was the learning that the automotive industry needed to change the way cars were powered, not just sold, and that was the beginning of the journey for the entrepreneur to venture into the energy sector to create environmentally sustainable power sources. As he learned through his journey, he started following the ensuing rule:

"There can be no profit without a well-defined purpose."

The point of mentioning Richard Branson and his take on success is to remind you that failure is just as important as success is. Naturally, humans try to hide things that embarrass them while telling the world about the good stuff they have achieved. But the truth is that the good does not come unless you go through the bad and the ugly. Failed experiences can either only be setbacks you face, or they can be life lessons. It is up to you to decide what you do with your life. Entrepreneur and business Richard Branson could have given up after multiple letdowns or learned from his mistakes and persist in the market and did the latter. In his own words:

"I believe in our resourcefulness and in our capacity to invent solutions to the problems we have ourselves created."

Failure and My Journey

If I were to talk about where I think I failed, I would definitely say that my personal life took a great hit. Looking back, it makes sense that it did because I had to learn to be a family man before thinking about pursuing and maintaining a personal, romantic relationship. The way I see it, the direction in which you put your energy, you are bound to succeed. Be it personal, professional, mental, emotional, or physical health. In life, we are meant to constantly work on things that will help us grow. As human beings fight against the time war, we come to understand that we eventually outgrow places, people, and even older versions of ourselves. And the truth is, if this did not happen, evolution and probably revolution would not have been possible. We would still be stuck in the ways of our ancestors, and there would be no point in existing.

Every year, the rotations and orbits of the earth give rise to different seasons, reminding us that everything is bound to grow and die as life continues. The fact that even time that moves on does not come back is the biggest, clearest evidence of the fact that you have limited opportunities, and when failure comes your way, it, too, will pass. Getting up and falling back down are two sides of the same coin. The only difference is that we give up once we get to the other side. Oftentimes, we do not even want to acknowledge or accept that there is another side.

While success and achievements teach you what you are good at, setbacks teach you where you can improve rather than making you weaker. How will you know where you need to improve unless you fall down to find out?

One of my biggest disappointments is that I failed to provide a safe and secure environment for my family. As much as I tried to be there for my children through my marriages, I wish I had known the ropes of marital relationships before I got into them. Although my parents had a healthy marriage, as did Daddy John, in this arena, I did take a while to learn what life was teaching me.

My constant reaction to losing any of my wives worked. Drowning myself in my profit and loss sheets, balance sheets, and strategy decks made me feel like I was in control, and I would obsess over trying to get things right, especially when I felt alone. Although I fought to keep my children with me and close to their mothers, it would have really helped had I known how to make my marriages work in the first place. But I did my best then, and that is something that keeps me satisfied.

In some situations, there is only so much we can do, and then it is up to the universe to keep us going. You see, no matter what you are going through, you will come to find that other people around you have it worse. Be it the failure of a business, the ending of a marriage, or the loss of a child as was my fate; someone has it worse. And sometimes, all you can do is try to make things better for someone else to get through your own pain.

If I were to speak of my blunders through my seventy-four years of life, I could print multiple books under my name, but the point is not to fill out pages with things that are bound to happen. The goal is to find the learning through every experience, and that is the true way you can help someone else, through advice, experiences, and, well, an autobiography. How you feel and what you are going through does not give you the right to bring others down. Accept the help you need and move on. Some people might help you get through your difficulties if you let them, while not everyone will push you to recovery, and that is fine. As long as you are honest to those people around you and to yourself, without hurting anyone, you should be able to make this world a slightly better place. Being a positive influence in the world starts with being positive and truthful to yourself, regardless of what you feel, because no one will speak your truth for you. It is your responsibility to pick yourself up, dust yourself off, and put yourself in the saddle.

Maintaining a steady pace and sticking to it will give you insight into your own abilities and shortcomings. Consistency is key, and they don't just say that. Being patient, giving a situation its due time to fully manifest, using clarity and focus through your experiences, and perseverance will help you build meaningful habits that will help you prosper through life. You will experience discipline and self-control aligning themselves with your core values while you begin to trust and take pride in your own decisions. The higher you experience these principles, the faster you will be on track to self-development. You will find yourself accepting more accountability, responsibly taking up on tasks better for you, and you will also notice people looking up to you.

If you have stuck with me so far, can you think of one person in my life who reminds me after reading everything mentioned above? That's right! It's my

Daddy John. The more resilient and observant he was, the further he got in life. Not only that, but he would also not jump to conclusions instantly when things did not go his way, and I think this strengthened his problem-solving ability. The key is to achieve the goal even if the route changes.

The way I would advise younger people to embrace failures and turn them into your successes is to change their mindset. In life, you are like a tightrope walker. These walkers carry a long pole that they balance straight through their walk. Now imagine that one side of that pole are people, and on the other side are tasks, responsibilities, and duties. If you fall off the tightrope, you die. That is not as difficult sometimes as it is to stay on the challenging narrow path below your feet, keeping everything perfectly in place. Your task is to balance the rope – the relationships and the responsibilities. If you lean too much on people to get things done, you will tip the pole on one end, off-balancing yourself and your life. And if you focus too much on your responsibilities, you will end up losing the important people in your life, depicted by the rope tilting in the other position.

Your purpose in life may vary from other people, but no matter who you come across, they are all walking the same tightrope, maybe at different paces. At some points in life, your tasks need more attention, while other times, you need to fulfill your responsibility as a social being. Whatever the need may be, learning to balance is crucial if you want to get to the end safely.

The reason *ALL* of my marriages failed, without a doubt, was that I was too busy working, making money. I needed a partner at all those points in my life that I got married but maybe not a spouse, or so I think. I did not realize it, but I was not ready for the commitment. Unfortunately, or fortunately, life had other plans for me, and that is something I had to go through to be the man I am today. Either way, I have no regrets because all those experiences made me the man I am today. See? We all learn to point out the bright side of things. It is all a matter of time that it happens.

Embrace failure, Ensure Success

The bottom line is that you need to learn to take the good with the bad. You cannot always be selective with the outcomes of your experiences, especially if you are trying out new things. Once you get a handle on life, you will start to see a pattern on how to go about things, but even then, favorable outcomes are not guaranteed. Some instances that feel like the end of the world are only the beginning of good times in your life. Either way, it is your mindset that will help you get through life. To be a successful entrepreneur and person in life, you have to get through difficult times with just the courage and positivity as you celebrate the good times in life. Of course, you need time to grieve and get through tough times, but once you do, you have to promise yourself never to look back.

Important Takeaways

1. Realize The Importance of Failure

Excuse me for sounding like a broken record, but sometimes those do a much better job than just some words on a piece of paper. You will never realize the importance of white without black and vice versa. The strength of black is only recognized when it is compared to a palette of different colors. Similarly, to recognize the different struggles of your life, you have to *go through* the struggles, to begin with. If you always want to be successful and reap fruits, you may as well just repeat the things you have always done in life. If you are okay with not experiencing growth, you may opt not to say anything, do anything, and feel anything. But as human beings, we are bound to want prosperity in our lives. Just observe a small child trying to walk for the first time. The transitionary phase comes with multiple times of falling down until one day, the falling stops.

2. Your Failure Is Your Teacher

That is right. While success is there to take the edge of the hard work you have put in, setbacks exist to remind you of how much growing you have left to do. Look at it through an open mind. This means more experiences, more meeting new people if required, and more learning about yourself. The best relationship you will ever foster and nurture will be the one you will have with yourself, and what is better than watering your own soil, watching your leaves grow green, and your flowers bloom. The gratitude and appreciation you will have for yourself once you have gone through something that seemed impossible at first will have you respect yourself in new-found ways. Cherish life, and it is up and downs – it is truly what will take you higher.

3. Balance Is Crucial

Whether it be a healthy lifestyle or personal and professional relationships, learning to balance is always going to be the most important thing you will learn in life. The series of events that will take place in your life will never be in order, but it is up to you to make sense of them. You may welcome a baby in the world the same day you endure a loss in your business. Do you celebrate your happiness or frown upon your loss? The decision is yours, but you cannot blame people for the things that happen to you. As long as you try your best to strike a balance, you will be fine.

4. Failure and Success Go Hand-in-Hand

Just as your shadow follows you everywhere you go, failures will follow your success and vice versa. If you find yourself stressing over a failure you have endured, try to float above the grief and understand what your situation is trying to teach you. More often than not, failure will be your first step, but second will be step two. How do you know this fact? Well, you don't. But not knowing is not a good enough reason to quit when things get tough. If you are not your own partner in crime to get through the difficulties in life, no one will help you. Through failing businesses and drifting family members, you are your truest friend. Trust yourself so you can trust those around you.

I would like to quote a small poem on failure and success I often think of when I encounter a setback in life.

Once upon a time,

Success asked failure,

Why do you exist when I am the ultimate result of those who work hard?

Failure said,

I am the one who keeps them coming back to get to you

Success says,

But successful people always keep trying till they get it right

Failure smiles and says,

How do you expect them to get it right if they don't do it wrong first?

~

Brian Bonar

CHAPTER 7:

LOVE AND WAR

How does Love speak?
In the faint flush upon the telltale cheek,
And in the pallor that succeeds it; by
The quivering lid of an averted eye–
The smile that proves the parent to a sigh
Thus doth Love speak.
How does Love speak?
By the uneven heart-throbs, and the freak
Of bounding pulses that stand still and ache,
While new emotions, like strange barges, make
Along vein-channels their disturbing course;
Still as the dawn, and with the dawn's swift force–
Thus doth Love speak.
How does Love speak?
In the avoidance of that which we seek–
The sudden silence and reserve when near–
The eye that glistens with an unshed tear–
The joy that seems the counterpart of fear,
As the alarmed heart leaps in the breast,
And knows, and names, and greets its godlike guest–
Thus doth Love speak.
How does Love speak?
In the proud spirit suddenly grown meek–
The haughty heart grown humble; in the tender
And unnamed light that floods the world with splendor;
In the resemblance which the fond eyes trace
In all fair things to one beloved face;
In the shy touch of hands that thrill and tremble;

In looks and lips that can no more dissemble–
Thus doth Love speak.
How does Love speak?
In the wild words that uttered seem so weak
They shrink ashamed in silence; in the fire
Glance strikes with glance, swift flashing high and higher,
Like lightnings that precede the mighty storm;
In the deep, soulful stillness; in the warm,
Impassioned tide that sweeps through throbbing veins,
Between the shores of keen delights and pains;
In the embrace where madness melts in bliss,
And in the convulsive rapture of a kiss –
Thus doth Love speak.

~

Ella Wheeler Wilcox

Ever since we were little, we have been told to follow certain rules and regulations. When a child is born, the mother looks after this little person, feeds him, clothes him, bathes him, and takes care of him every step of the way till he can actually take his steps. When he gets older, his father teaches him everything he knows. His beliefs, how the world works and helps shape his exterior. The parents, together, make sure they provide him with everything in the world so he can be a wise man, make his own decisions, and hopefully, have his own family someday.

As he grows up and goes to school, he starts learning different values from different children. He learns to express himself in a controlled environment, interact with his peers, and learn the wonders of the world through his books and class activities. He learns a certain order of things. This child, who his parents have put so much time and energy into, is always going to be their pride and joy, and they begin to set their expectations out of his life. He works hard, goes to college, and further explores ideas, and meets new people that further open up his mind. He goes to parties to find people similar to him. Life is good. He starts discussing ideas, having meaningful conversations, and making important life choices, such as where he sees himself in five years. He chooses his major accordingly, if his fate has not been sealed by his parents, and pursues this path.

Somewhere along the lines, he comes across a beautiful girl that he falls in love with at first sight. She is perfect. Tall, slender, and smart. She has a smile that is brighter than the sun, and he instantly knows she is the one. As he thinks about being the big businessman in his professional life, he also asks her to be his wife, and they get married after they graduate college. They move into a cute house together, guarded by a picket fence, and they have two cars parked in their driveway. Soon enough, they find out they are expecting their first child, and they are both over the moon. All their lives now change to welcome this new person on Earth, altering their plans. Now, they have to constantly think about how they can nurture their love in the form of this little baby.

A few years down the line, they have two perfect children that are starting middle school and high school, respectively, and the couple is now middle-aged. They have fixed routines where they spend time together on weekends, whereas weekdays are all about making sure they get to work on time and the kids get all their homework done. Another few years, and the first child is off to college. The man who was once himself just a boy is now looking at hefty college bills just so his child can get prime education and live life to the fullest. He works day and night just so he can offer his kids the best life. He, too, has expectations from his children just like his parents did with him.

His interests have now changed. Parties have changed into occasional parent-teacher meetings, and instead of discussing new ideas, he discusses current political and economic views with other fathers he has had to befriend to make sure he knows the people his children are hanging out with. Time goes on, and routines take up most days. His wife is his companion, and most days, the two just want some peace and quiet in life.

A few more years and his age have not been too kind to him. Arthritis keeps him up most nights while his wife struggles most days because she can barely sustain enough energy to remember enough details to get through the day. The two often sit out at the front porch, talking about the good old days. They enjoy vacations because that is when the family – their children and grandchildren – come together. They enjoy feasts and festivities, but it only lasts so long. Grandpa and Grandma now look forward all year long to seeing their offspring. Soon enough, their grandchildren stop visiting because they are busy with their lives, much like the ones they spent a few years ago when they were young.

Everything that is mentioned above is probably not the exact way you will live life, but the cycle of life is vicious and beautiful alike. Generally, you will have more bad days than good ones. You will not fall in love at first sight, and love will never be enough to get you through a relationship forever. Feelings do not sustain relationships. Most days, you will be running after a clock to get things done. Your spouse will throw a tantrum first thing in the morning when you turn around in bed to give them a kiss. When you leave your room, your children will take forever to get out of bed before you drop them off at school, only to realize that the activity of taking care of your little ones has shaved off significant minutes off your preparation time. You may have to skip breakfast or speed up you are dressing up process to make it to work on time. When you once again step into the same four walls for the next eight or so hours, you will probably be greeted by the boss questioning your punctuality when the reality is far from what meets the eye.

When you get on and busy with your life, you will realize how different things are personally and professionally. No movies, books, or shows can ever tell you what is about to come your way. Your relationship with your spouse has never existed and, hence, can never be defined for you. You will have to work every single day to make things work. It is mutual values and belief systems that help two people build and connect with each other and move forward, and not just love. Sure, it is good to share the love with your spouse, it will make your journey sweeter, but it is not the main ingredient that will give your marriage the essence it requires. You need trust, respect, compromise, and sacrifice, among many other intangibles, to make your marriage work.

Commitment to your spouse and your new life will intensify the partnership you both share. If you are looking to make things work long-term, you need to know that you will have to commit day or night to make a difference. Of course, there is no one way to do this. But remember, communication is crucial between two people. Now that you two share a bond, you have to honor it for life to be smooth. Keeping things to yourself and not talking about what works for you or them is going to start creating gaps in your relationship. And whether you like it or not, the more you wait to bring things out in the open, the deeper the void will get, and the foundation will become weak. The relation you once had will be long gone, and the two of you will lose sight of the people you used to be.

Clarity between two people leads to effective conflict resolution that is important to establish a healthy bond. Avoiding contempt, accepting constructive criticism, and overcoming stress is all possible as long as couples understand each other. Leaving each other alone after arguments, yelling, and gaslighting may satisfy your ego, but at the end of the day, both parties lose their bond for good, and if children are involved, they suffer the most. Spouses in healthy marriages never use abusive language with each other or otherwise. Abusive gestures – mental, emotional, verbal, or physical – in order to gain control of the situation or satisfy oneself is a dead-end road. Children should never be at the receiving end of bad parental habits and generational curses. It is not their fault that you do not get along with your spouse. You get to choose your life partner, but they did not choose their parents.

Spouses who indulge in intimacy are more likely to be kind to each other. Emotional or physical intimacy builds trust, respect, and support between two people in marriage, which are important wheels to keep the wagon going. It also promotes healthy friendship between couples, helping them learn about how their partner is growing into their role. It is important that the two know each other as they age in their relationships. Human beings outgrow themselves and their definitive roles, and it is only fair to bring your spouse along on that journey. Getting comfortable with each other's company will become easier if you know how and why your partner is behaving a certain way.

Whenever children are in the picture, parents need to realize that their relationship has extended to that of dependents. Bringing children along and helping them understand their individual personalities is an enriching experience they deserve. Children tend to be more friendly with parents who have open communication with their little ones, accept their mistakes, and admit to being human. Remember, you are older than them but not perfect. In fact, the sooner your children know you do not have a map for navigation through parenthood, the more open their communication and understanding will be toward you.

Realizing that – even though you have life knocking at your door every step of every day – your partner is still a human being who needs your attention will make your marriage stronger as you proceed. Take time to appreciate each other, go out often even though you have children, and find ways to do things the other person loves to make them feel special. This does not have to be huge. It can be as much as getting your wife a rose once a week. As long as you put in the effort, you can be assured that it will materialize.

Alone time is key because you can express your feeling without feeling judged or offending the kids. Your spouse might understand your problems, but sometimes, your children might not comprehend your standpoint. Maintain boundaries and make sure the two of you maintain transparency and privacy in the way you do things. It is okay to disagree and maybe even display your frustration so long as you stay within your limits of trust and disrespect. Seeing the human side of your partner often will make you realize that they are, in fact, human and make forgiveness easier for them. You are perfectly capable of hurting your partner and vice versa. But it is important to healthily deal with your feelings as they happen because keeping them inside will only push you to keep bringing up the past over and over again.

When it was time for me to settle down for the first time, I knew who I wanted to be with. Patricia, my first wife, was my best friend, and we grew up in the same town together. We started dating as we grew up, and soon after, we said our vows and tied the knot. We were happy when things began. It was safe. We were in a place we had always known, with the person who we knew, and close to home. But growth does not come from things that feel safe, does it? And well, knowing Brian Bonar by now, you must have guessed that it was not enough for me. My relationship started before I was recruited and selected by IBM. I mean, sure, I was still working, but you know my complicated start with the company by now. Patricia and I welcomed our first child within a year of our marriage. I had also become part of an important team by now and was motivated to keep going ahead. Soon enough, IBM was sending me to deal with important clients and execute important projects all over the world. I visited France, Germany, and Italy – just to name a few countries – and that is when I really started seeing the world up close. It opened my eyes. I began to like traveling. I started realizing my potential, and the people around me encouraged me to go further.

This growth in my professional life, however, meant that my wife was running the show at home all on her own, and it drove a wedge in our relationship. A few months later, our small drift turned into a full-fledged divorce. I used to think that marriage was two people performing their own roles in their own capacities but little did I know those gender roles were a thing of the past even back then. You know how sometimes you see something happen right in front of your eyes, yet you cannot move fast enough to grab it. One of those dreams where your feet won't move no matter how fast you try to run? Well, that is what happened with my marriage firsthand, and I could not do much to stop it. Not only would it not work at that time, but there was also a part of me that slowly began to realize that I did not want it to. Don't get me wrong, my wife and I had a really good bond as friends, but as a couple, we did not go well together. For the next few months to come, we worked on getting a divorce because I could not wait to go and explore the world. I was excited, and there was nothing that was going to hold me back. I do not want to sound like a horrible person, but we were not compatible. She was a routine, organized individual, and I like to dive headfirst into untested waters. Sure, it worked in my career, but my personal life needed much more growth from me.

Although my first marriage failed, I kept my heart open to love. I can recall a funny story from a few years ago when my ex-wife and current wife were together. We were at the Cayman Islands with Patricia on my left and my existing wife on my right. They bonded with each other so well that they both asked me to leave so they could talk about something personal with each other. All my kids know each other, and they hang out; there is no bad blood there. But standing here after all these years, I realize that sometimes it is just the person you don't get along with in a specific setting. So far, all my wives are great women, good friends, and exceptional mothers, but we just did not get along as married people.

Life becomes easier once you realize who you are as a person and what personally works for you. After all my experiences, I have come to realize that working on yourself should come alongside working on your career, or you will go through heartbreak and disappointment till you get it right. At different points in my life, I needed different things, but I was unsure what they were. It took me a lot of figuring out situations on my own to know who I am and what sits well with me. While I do not regret my experiences, I do wish I would have given myself the same time and priority I did to my job and career back then.

Not too long ago, my first wife fell and broke her ankle. I made sure she was okay and would call her to check up on her every chance I got. She is a tough one. I will give you that because she took care of our kids after we were divorced. When I see her strength and her resilience, it gives me a sort of hope to keep going in life. Our bond and friendship are what keep us going.

At the age of forty years old, I got married for the second time, and I thought I had found my panacea. Had someone told me that it wouldn't work when I settled down with Linda, I would have probably laughed at them. But, well, hindsight is twenty-twenty, and it did, in fact, happen. I have no regrets because I would not be happily married right now if that did not happen. She was a gorgeous woman and someone incredibly smart. We had fun while it lasted, but once again, she cheated on me with someone else, and that was the end of that.

Through it all, I always tried to be there for my kids. I have said this once before, and I will say it again because it is something that I believe in; your children do not deserve to bear the brunt of your non-functional relationship. Children do not understand the nature of the relationship between two married people, and seeing their guardians fighting confuses them. Whatever I went through, I stuck with my children thoroughly because I knew they did not deserve what was coming their way.

Did You Know?

Divorce is as confusing and challenging for children as it is for adults. While parents think about the how's, where's, who's, when's, and why's, the children who are probably going to less of one or both parents are worried about coping with the loss or absence. Experts say that the first year of divorce is the toughest, especially for the kids. Often, they do not know how to react or respond to the situation and end up with repressed feelings of distress, frustration, anger, and anxiety. Although in the long-term, it is better for the family to dismantle if the relationship is dysfunctional, at the moment, this solution does not seem to be the right one. For most kids, getting through the first year is the major challenge, after which they find it relatively easier to accept the rather unfavorable situation.

When young children find out about their parents getting a divorce, they get severely emotionally distressed. They struggle to understand what is happening, why they have to visit different homes, and even fail to comprehend how their parents can have different partners. Experts say that young children see their parents as loving, guiding figures who they can depend on. When their relationship ends, children begin to perceive that they, too, will one day be on the receiving end of a relationship that ended because of the death of love. Children mimic their parents and innately believe that they are the perfect beings in the world. When something unpleasant happens to their idols, they start assuming the same for themselves, too.

Children who are of the grade school age group perceive divorce a little more differently. These kids are growing up and beginning to make more mistakes.

Somewhere along the lines, they begin to think that failure on their part is the reason their parents are breaking up. See here, too, that they still think highly of their parents, taking the blame for the wedge that broke their marriage. Sometimes, these kids carry the burdensome yet incorrect belief that they could have done something better to help their parents.

When teenagers have to watch their parents go through a divorce, they often find themselves angry at the situation they cannot control. It changes their perception about marriage, and they find it rather convenient to blame one parent for the loss of the relationship rather than viewing it as a team failure. They end up with feelings of resentment, loss of control, and hatred towards one parent because this helps them hold someone accountable in their heads, at least.

In most cases, it is the father that loses touch with the children and vice versa. A decrease in contact time with the parents leads to a weakened bond and deteriorating relationship, increasing stress levels in both individuals. For other children, it is not the divorce that is the difficult part but the negative stressors that come after. Naturally, such feelings of negativity result in children developing mental health problems from a young age that affect their growth as healthy individuals. Their view of relationships changes, triggering an adjustment order in the children that sometimes leads to commitment issues when it comes to personal relationships in the future.

Children who come from divorced families exhibit various behavioral problems that are problematic for them and those around them. Such children manifest externalizing issues such as impulsion, delinquency, erratic behavior, and indulging in conflicts with no apparent reason. This also leads to poor academic performances and the adoption of behaviors that are risky, to begin with, just for the sake of seeking a thrill, for instance, substance and alcohol abuse. According to a study, children who have problematic parents who get divorced before the child turns five are at a higher risk of initiating sexual activity at young ages.

It is extremely common for children to repress their emotions, thinking that the situation will be okay, without expressing what they actually want. They try not to upset their parents, be the cause of further discourse, and sometimes, they simply do not understand how to deal with the situation. Many times, they are absorbed with grief and sadness to the point that they do not know what to make of the situation. Divorce can have a huge impact on kids' self-esteem, and as research shows, a decrease in quality time with parents leads to a decelerated standard of living and gives rise to the frequency of tense situations between the members. As these children grow up, they continue to exhibit psychological difficulties, going in and out of unfulfilling relationships, sometimes looking to mend what their parents' marriage might have taken away from them. The saddest reality is that such kids themselves may go through the devastating process of divorce themselves.

When adults get joint custody of the child, he or they may feel like a messenger between the parents. While the parents may use the child as a medium to communicate their messages, the child often wonders why they have to be stuck in such a situation in the first place. A concept called 'inappropriate disclosures' comes into play where the parents discuss a situation with the kid rather than a friend. While this often happens when the parent with custody feels helpless, the resulting feelings that a child goes through can lead them to feel torn. In such cases, sometimes, the child feels pressured to grow up and take care of the parent. Children of divorced individuals see their parents as emotionally vulnerable beings and automatically step up to be the person they have looked up to all these years.

Children respond to situations such as the conflict in three major ways. Experts say that these reactions are basically what their bodies feel because they are often too young to understand what is happening when their parents are getting divorced. Even if the proceeding is completely civil, children sometimes tend to feel and exhibit negative emotions. One major way kids respond to divorce situations is avoidance. Human beings, in general, find it easy to shut everything out, to protect themselves from what they are feeling. They assume it is easier because, in the meantime, they do not have to deal with the situation. Sometimes, kids who do this have good intentions. They are trying to act brave for their parents, even trying to protect them in tough times. It is a natural reaction, but the underlying cause can either be positive or negative. However, if the parents do not open up with their kids and explain to them what is going on, the child's true feelings will never be known.

Kids also normally show aggression in the situation. As discussed, these are usually much older kids, such as teenagers or adolescents, who are beginning to make sense of the world. Not having control of the situation can often lead them to mimic the tension in the household, lashing out at the parents themselves or those around them. They may not understand their feelings of frustration themselves, but their coping mechanisms get activated to protect them from getting hurt. And you know what they say, *the best defense is a good offense.*

In some cases – very few of them – children act maturely enough to confront their parents, and this is the most effective method to deal with conflict. This happens only with selective children who are older and have acquired the competence to deal with their parents with emotional maturity.

Helping Your Kids

The challenge lies for the parents to ensure that their relationship has a minimal spillover effect on the children. But what can parents do? First and foremost, they need to explain and listen to their children.

The two people going through the divorce have been grieving their relationship for months or years before the actual legal process takes place, but the children have not. Parents should be honest with their kids about what is happening, how it will affect them in the long term, and how things will go about from the current point onwards. You do not need to necessarily sit down and have a super long conversation with them, but the key is, to be honest. Every moment you spend with your kids, even at this point, will contribute toward building a bond with them. And frankly, if you want to raise good, honest individuals, you need to set an example for them first.

Another important skill to learn is the ability to co-parent your child peacefully. When parents engage in excessive conflict, the level of distress in children also increases. Screaming, yelling, and using bad language are linked with bad behavior in the children who express this kind of tension in the house. How successfully parents can help their kids through the transition process determines how successfully the child will adjust to the newness that is to follow. Parents can also seek therapy and the help of other professionals to get through the painful process of divorce.

It is also important for the two exes to discuss major tasks such as dropping and picking the kids, homework responsibility, kids' meal times, and so on before the divorce is final. These responsibilities can be revisited once the emotional tension around the process settles, but it is the initial turmoil that makes or breaks the situation. The ex-partners must also give each other some room to act like parents, putting their emotional grudges our feelings aside. If your relationship is good enough, a little appreciation for your partner will also go a long way. When adults work together and make judgments based on rationality, they end up making much better decisions for the kids in the long term.

Divorce is going to put your child through a lot of emotional and mental distress. They might lose friends, say goodbye to their favorite teacher, and even make peace with the fact that their favorite parent might not always be around in case a change of geographical location is involved. It is never a good idea to cut ties off completely. Try to make sure that the kids are still in touch with their favorite aunt or get to see their distant best friend enough, so they do not feel left out. When children blame you for losing their friends and relationships, they most likely carry this feeling in their hearts and maintain grudges.

When my relationships ended, I took custody of all my children, except for the kids in my first marriage. I was too young and fresh to take care of them. But after that, I made sure that my children's needs were met, and I often also shifted houses to ensure that the kids were close to their mothers. Understanding the mother-child relationship was of utmost importance to me, and I never did anything to hurt that sacred bond. In fact, I tried that my divorces were swift and as bloodless as possible, so the children would not have to deal with traumatic experiences for the rest of their lives. The way you deal with the first few months after the divorce is crucial because this is when everyone is learning to adjust to new schedules. It will take some time for things to go back to normal again but as long as everyone is willing to work toward a peaceful goal, rest assured, it will happen.

When you are in a marriage that has given you kids, it is not as easy for you to get out. It takes a lot to accept your responsibility and even more to live up to these duties. In a nutshell, children suffer the most out of a broken marriage, and it is up to the parents to create a smooth, transitionary environment for these kids and to ensure that their relationship with their spouse does not take down the children with it. It is easier to make a parenting plan, where you and your spouse discuss things beforehand for yourselves and the children alike. It is easy to hate each other and lose focus, but your kids never have to bear the brunt of your bitterness.

Summarizing everything said in this chapter, the key points to keep with you are:

1. Marriage works on trust, respect, and compromise. If you expect to be taken care of, you will have to put in an equal amount of time and effort. As long as you can find the perfect balance between personal and professional life, you will be able to work towards a successful relationship with your partner. Sometimes, you have to put in one hundred and fifty per cent and only expect back a hundred per cent, and find a partner who holds the same values as you. Guaranteed, you will find happiness in such a case.

2. There is no one-size-fits-all solution to work around your life and relationships. You have to pave your own way through your life and

make the best out of what you have. Your life is not like anyone else's; hence, you are the best navigator of your ship through life. The best thing you can do is enjoy your experiences and make the most out of them with the people you love.

3. Be honest with your kids when it comes to the kind of relationship you have with your spouse. They are individuals who deserve the truth, and putting them through your troubles is not fair to them. You get to choose your spouse, but they cannot pick their parents. Hence, they deserve your respect enough for you to tell them about how their life will also change because of your relationship with your partner.

4. Repressing your feelings or having children suppress their feelings about the end of your marriage is not fair. When children repress their emotions, they lose their ability to healthily express themselves and sometimes permanently. Having a healthy conversation with your children is crucial as a two-way relationship will establish a boundary of trust between you two.

5. Help your children understand what you are going through because they are not mature enough to understand themselves. Children

are deeply affected but sometimes not mentally developed enough to comprehend what is happening with them. It is your responsibility as an adult to stand up and be your voice of reason through the process of your separation and post-divorce.

6. Both parents are important for a child to lead a healthy life. Parents must work together to ensure that the children go through their life healthily. When children imprint on the animosity that parents have for each other, they mimic it, and usually, one parent is on the receiving end of the negativity. Hence, whatever you do as a couple must be broken down and explained to your young ones.

7. And lastly, make sure you learn from your past experiences so you do not end up making the same mistake over and over. When things go south, your responsibility is to understand what went wrong rather than thinking it was not meant for you.

CHAPTER 8:

DON'T HOLD BACK

When I was conducting research for this book, I chuckled when I Googled the meaning of 'happiness,' and you will understand why when you look up the definition as well. Happiness is a highly subjective concept with the common understanding of eliminating the sad bits out of life. What do you think of when you think about being happy? Do you see yourself in your favorite place on Earth? Perhaps with loved ones? Or do you merely think about having a fancy house and a brand-new car? Whatever your visualization of happiness may be, know that it is a concept solely yours, and people do whatever they can to attain their happiness.

Experts and research have shown that people who go after happiness from material fulfillment attain contentment only for a short period of time. And it makes sense because if happiness or fulfillment does not come from within, it will never be satisfied. The more you seek worldly things, the hungrier you will get, and the void inside you will also get deeper.

Happiness can be viewed as being in a state of contentment. This shows us that happiness is not a trait one possesses. Rather it is a state of mind. It fluctuates given the situation ahead of us and is not a permanent feature. Happiness is roughly defined as a state of contentment and pleasure but is different from other feelings such as joy, bliss, and ecstasy. You can either feel happiness or show that you are happy. Either way, it is both an internal and an external experience. There is no set definition of happiness, and people experience multiple situations and events where they find pleasure and contentment.

Professors and experts have also tried to quantify and identify what happiness constitutes. After putting in years of work, researchers Ed Diener, Chu Kim-Prieto, and their colleagues in 2005 showed us three main ways which positive psychology used to approach happiness:

- An assessment of life and all its facets is called happiness

- When past emotional experiences have culminated, they define happiness

- Happiness is a summary of several emotional reactions over time

Although researchers more or less agree on what happiness is and what it feels like – satisfaction with life and gaining pleasure out of your circumstances – they are still struggling to figure out the scope or depth of happiness. Of course, given the subjectivity and personalization of the feeling, it is a no-brainer that it is not easy to identify or define happiness.

Experts who carried out research to reveal what happiness is deduced that there are certain factors that decide the level of our happiness. These include:

- Level of income
- Physical health
- Social relationships
- Moral values
- Familial relationships
- Positive emotions
- Labor market status

While these factors play a major role in other experiences in life, the most important aspect of happiness is the relationships we have with people around us, such as our significant others, parents, siblings, and our friends. The stronger and healthier these relationships, the happier we will be. Human beings optimize their bonds and connections by seeking pleasure within them. Contentment comes from getting what you put into relationships because fulfillment that comes out of relationships is a two-way road, and we are all looking for love and acceptance along the way.

According to studies, human beings can learn to be happier in life. As long as you keep the door to individual improvement open, you will allow yourself to expand into the idea of happiness because it is a fluid concept without any boundaries or equations. The best way to increase your happiness is to list down a series of things that make you happy and put in the effort to enhance the quality of your experiences. Taking it one day at a time will help you reflect on what you truly need to work on, attributing to overall happier life.

Richard Branson on Happiness

"I truly believe that 'stuff' really does not bring happiness."

Richard Branson often talks about the rich relationship he has fostered and nurtured throughout his life. Even though he stands at a whopping net worth of $4 billion, he believes that meaning and depth in life come from family, friends, good health, and making a positive difference in the world. Given his family background already, his intention was never to get rich, and it makes sense because of the abundance of wealth that was available at his disposal. Branson says that he aimed to always have a positive impact in the world through his business. He, indeed, made a difference given his many business ventures and, to date, teaches his children his personal values and beliefs.

This one time, his wife Joan and Richard were on a houseboat that sank, taking down all their possessions with it. However, the only thing the couple missed out of everything was the family photo albums they held so close to them. Branson believes happiness in personal life leads to productivity at the workplace and vice versa. He believes in the value and power of good relationships and says that by nurturing the connections around us, we become mentally healthy and happy. Branson's ideology can be seen as he practices what he preaches at work. By putting his employees first, he trusts them to retain their customers because the best way someone does a good job is when they feel appreciated. Branson realizes his position as a boss and a leader and what he can do with it. He encourages his coworkers and makes sure they feel taken care of so they can perform better, increasing overall productivity and efficiency.

According to Richard, there are a few ways in which you can work to increase the quality of your relationships. It is important to realize that you will move in the direction that you put the effort in. Whether it be personal relationships or professional ones, you will be able to nurture wherever you put your effort.

- Make time for each other. The most important thing one can do is be there for another person when the need arises. Set some time aside for either your family or your employees, and spend time with them. The true meaning of happiness will come when everyone around you is happy, too, as opposed to when you just focus on yourself. Of course, focusing on your goals is important as well, but the bigger picture should always be to create an environment of pleasure and contentment.

- Hear your loved ones out. Listening is an important skill that will take you far with the people that matter the most to you. Showing empathy and attentiveness can sometimes be all one needs. When someone is talking to you, it is your duty to listen to them intently and with compassion. Remember, it is about them, not you. When you value the words of those you love, they will value you back, and sometimes, happiness is a simple, deep talk with someone you love.

- Act on your words. Once you know what is going on in someone's life, you can decide what to do to make them feel better. If your friend is stressed or you're your brother is going through a breakup, take them out for a meal or drinks and help them get out of their painful state of mind. Think about ways in which you can lighten someone's burden to make life a little easier for them.

It is the simplest things that create an impact in the lives of people. Be it a simple hug or a small present, the right gesture at the right time can help brighten their day and strengthen your bond. When the people around you are happy and content, you will automatically feel their positive energy grow around the room and circle back to you. The thing about the energy that humans possess is that it can always be transferred. The more we give out, the more we get back. Hence, it is important to spread positivity yet minimize the negativity by sharing your pain. Richard Branson has eight key pieces of advice that he uses to promote happiness and contentment in his personal and professional life.

- Success is never measured by the amount of money you make. And it is true because once you start spending, you will then become miserable because the dollars you have pitted against your content state of mind will begin to diminish. Richard Branson assures us that as long as we are chasing the bigger purpose of making each other's lives better, the money will follow. He wrote on his LinkedIn that people often think that an entrepreneur's main goal is to make money. However, this is not correct. As long as you keep striving for more in terms of your goal, you will keep moving forward. If you focus on doing small things to make you happy, you will find success making its way to you. It is all about appreciating the little things you have.

- Personal touch is key. Richard Branson believes that nothing can compare to stripping down your gadgets once in a while to have a face-to-face conversation. The usage of technology has increased to no end, and even though our gadgets go everywhere with us, it is important that we put our devices aside and live in the moment. Branson focuses on the importance of the company of whoever you are with and to make the most of the experience. A little attention and hearing someone out can go a long way, proving to be better for our own mental health as well as the health of our relationships.

Richard Branson believes in being in the moment because once the moment is gone, it will never come back. He says that being alive is our biggest opportunity and soaking up the moment is our surest key to success, creating our little moments of happiness. Excessive device usage impacts our relationships, weakening our bonds, something we most definitely regret in the long run.

- Have fun with what you do. If you are not having fun, you are doing something wrong. Branson emphasizes the fact that people should not work to live; rather, they should live to work because work should be enjoyable. He encourages people to quit little habits and activities that are not fun because otherwise, they are a waste of time. Life on earth is limited, and people ought to do what serves their souls, rather than being stuck in dead-end jobs and poor relationships with people who are an added source of stress.

"Fun is one of the most important – and underrated – ingredients in any successful venture."

Richard Branson

- Spend time outdoors. Richard Branson encourages people to find hobbies that allow them to spend more time outdoors. Being outside is a great way to let go of all the stress and anxiety the gadgets can induce in us. Think of it as being drained by devices and recharging out with nature. Going hiking or trailing is a great way to boost your mood and give you more control of your circumstances. Additionally, physical exercises also stimulate the brain, energize the body, and feed the soul. Something as simple as walking your pet can leave you feeling refreshed, increasing your productivity, inducing feelings of happiness within you. So, get up, go out, and take time for yourself, your brain, and your body! We can all use a break from our busy lives to rejuvenate.

- Have big dreams. Richard Branson was only twenty-years-old when he launched Virgin Records and made a huge mark in the music industry. Despite people telling him that his plan was not practical or feasible, he took a chance and went ahead with it, and not too long after that. He was a major success. He dreamt big and followed through with it, pushing through the difficulties that followed. Branson says that it is our dreams which make us who we are, and if we do not dream, we are giving up on our own happiness. Our dreams are like the USP that set us apart from everyone else. The only difference between a dreamer and a believer is that a believer backs up his dream with work. He encourages everyone to take a chance on themselves and take risks to keep moving forward.

- Keep an open mind as you go. Richard Branson believes in the process of learning as you go through the process. Life is one big learning experience, and we should all always keep an open mind while taking on challenges that we think we will fail at. As someone who never went to university, Branson worked hard to get where he is, never ceasing the process of learning. He kept pushing through as he launched a number of ventures over many years, even in areas he had no previous experiences with. He believes that the key to learning firsthand is to dive headfirst into untested waters. Of course, you do need planning first, but that is a small part of the process. When he dove into new areas, he kept an open mind and learned as much as he could so he could apply those lessons to his new business ventures. And naturally, he did excel at some of his proceeding ventures.

Branson mentions it is this way that when you see an opportunity, you have to go for it. Even if it feels like it is not your area of expertise, you can always learn along the way. Focus on gaining skills as you go, taking up the chance to foster new connections, pushing yourself to make the most of the prospects ahead of you. He says that it does not matter if you do not know something because you can always learn. But the problem is when you treat your limited knowledge as a barrier to not growing. Branson encourages his followers to never give up and to seize opportunities. Self-doubt and second-guessing is the enemy of success and happiness. If you truly want to be happy, you need to keep taking chances to do things that might not always seem favorable. Playing safe will only teach you so many things, but risks will take you to a whole new level in terms of personal growth and development.

- Try new things fearlessly. Richard Branson is often known as the person who started young and never looked back. He has tried out new ideas and concepts and has built an empire of over two hundred companies. All his businesses are diverse and branched out, a testimony of Branson's personality itself. Branson is known to be an entrepreneur who asks everyone to push themselves till they get things done. It is not until you push yourselves out of your comfort zones that you will truly learn what you are capable of. Branson says that he has never achieved anything by being in his comfort zone. He advises all his followers to give up the first instance of the doubt when confronted with a challenge, wearing an 'I can' attitude, and face their difficulties head-on. If not, you will always ponder upon the 'what ifs' in life.

- Find happiness in every moment. Ensure that you dedicate every day to finding something positive each day. Happiness is not a consequence of success rather a state of mind that helps you focus on the good in life. When you do find success In life, happiness should come from within and act as a support system for when you achieve your milestones. Contrary to popular belief, Branson says that wealth and success did not bring him happiness. It was the other way round that he gained success and wealth because he found his happiness from within.

Richard Branson believes that happiness is always in front of you, waiting to be recognized. It is not a far-off goal, and that as much as you think it is far away, the harder it becomes to attain. Remember, dream big to be BIG!

CHAPTER 9:

MOVING FORWARD

B ecause of my entrepreneurial vision, I have traveled extensively around the globe. Last I checked, I had flown over six million miles using American Airlines, but that is not all. I also have more than a million and a half miles on United Airlines and another 750,000 miles on Delta. See, when you are an entrepreneur, you need to be constantly on the lookout for opportunities, and sometimes, that requires you to get out of the safe confines of your comfort zone. In today's world, business is changing rapidly, thanks to the development of innovative technologies and avant-garde business practices. The window of opportunity is short, and one wrong move can undo all of your hard work.

As one can imagine then, traveling has been a significant part of my life. Visiting foreign countries and making notes of how businesses operated there was a routine practice for me as an entrepreneur. Writing this, I cannot help but remember Daddy John. Had it not been for him, I would have never developed the courage and tenacity to get out of my safe space, explore alien lands, and learn to grow. As such, I owe a lot of gratitude to Daddy John for allowing me to inherit all of his entrepreneurial wisdom and acumen.

One thing that most people fail to realize is the importance of taking breaks. When you only focus on working, it tends to take a toll on your mental health, and then, taking a few weeks off is necessary for one to rejuvenate themselves. At the end of the day, we are all humans with real needs, wants, and desires, and therefore, one should feel no shame in taking some time for ourselves. See, our brains are similar to a battery, which need to be recharged. A vacation to a foreign land is the best way to provide your body with the rest and relaxation it rightly deserves.

For most people, taking a holiday to relax seems counterintuitive to their aims and ambitions, which frankly can not be farther from the truth. From my own experience, a break is exactly what one sometimes needs to get a fresh perspective. Plus, when we are stuck in a rigid schedule, we tend to run out of creative and innovative ideas. When that happens, taking a few days off of work to blow off steam can help one recover from the mental block that is inhibiting them from unleashing their true potential. I, for one, am all for vacations. As the saying goes, all work and no play makes Jack a dull boy.

There was a period in my life where I would fly from the States to Japan three days a week before traveling back again, and this cycle repeated itself for a considerable time. But every time I traveled, a recurring thought kept nagging the back of the head. See, when you visit a foreign land, you tend to visit its notable spots, stay in its hotels, try its traditional cuisines, and so on. But, are you really discovering the people of that country? I, for one, do not think so. At the end of your trip, you are still a tourist, with little to no knowledge about the inhabitants of that land.

Naturally, I was inclined to somehow find a way to build a real connection with the people hosting me. Over time, I developed a habit of making friends with the locals, which allowed me to get a deeper insight into their cultures, traditions, customs, and whatnot. To my surprise, what I came to discover was not at all what I had expected. I used to believe that the people of various countries were fundamentally different from each other. After all, isn't it the context that we experience, which molds our personality? If that is true, it makes sense for people born in different geographical zones to have different interests, beliefs, and values.

The reality, however, is that regardless of the differences in our language, religion, skin color, and nationality, we are one and the same. All of us are striving to accomplish a particular purpose, whatever that purpose might be. In that sense, each and every single person around the world is essentially the same. We function in the same way from the moment we are born to the moment we draw in our last breath. All of us wake up each morning, hoping to make our present better than our past. We stand groggily in front of a mirror and brush our teeth. We wash the sleep out of our eyes, put on make-up, comb our hair, and don fresh clothes. Before leaving for work, all of us have breakfast. Sure, the food we ingest differs, but it is all the same at the end of the day, isn't it?. We repeat the same routine five days a week, trying to build a better future for ourselves.

In fact, I would argue that we even share the same desires. We all long to have a partner who can be our rock as we traverse the murky waters of life. Most of us also want to have children and to give them the kind of luxuries we never got to experience. To summarize, then, we all share the same essence. That, perhaps, is the most important lesson I acquired through my years of visiting foreign lands and getting to know the people there.

At the end of the day, we are all mortals sent to Earth by a divine being, and we are simply waiting for him to call us back so we can get on with our next adventure. One of my fundamental beliefs is that there is indeed life after death. We might never find out what that life would be like, but I am positive that our souls do not simply disintegrate into nothingness after our death. I distinctly recall one of my experiences while I was in Acapulco, a city in Mexico. I was accompanied by a male friend, and we were using a voice app to communicate with the locals there. That is how we met Thomas, the bellman of the hotel we were staying at.

On a particularly rowdy night, my friend and I got so drunk that we could not even walk in a straight line. Thankfully, Thomas was there to help us. He escorted us from the pool to our bedrooms, where, after a short conversation, he extended us an invitation to visit his home. I was immediately taken aback by Thomas' kindness. After all, it is almost unheard of for a person to be willing to open his front door to a couple of drunk strangers. Before we left for his house, Thomas made us promise that we would not inform the hotel management about our little rendezvous because that could have gotten him fired for mixing in with the guests.

Eventually, we figured out a plan to meet with Thomas without alarming the hotel staff, and he took us to an alley behind the hotel that led to his house. Once we got there, I was awe-struck. His house was in a battered condition, with missing floors and washrooms with no running water. But there was a peacefulness in that quaint little Mexican town. My friend and I stayed there for some time, and everywhere we went, I could not help but take notice of the family values embedded deep within the people of that community. All people wanted to do there was share a beer, have a stimulating conversation before heading off to head with their kids cradled in their arms. Every person I encountered in that town seemed to be content and at peace with their lives.

That experience rocked me to my core. Not only did I feel humbled, but I also felt grateful for all of that I had. Only after meeting Thomas did I understand that one need not be wealthy to be successful, no. True happiness comes from within, and as long as you are content with your life, whether or not you are rich does not matter in the least. All humans contain a story within themselves, a fact which I realized after visiting Thomas's house. These stories deserve to be documented, but that is a privilege only afforded to a handful of people.

When you actually take the time to talk to people, you discover things that you would otherwise have never found out. People tend to feel hesitant about sharing details about their private lives, which frankly is understandable. No one appreciates it when a couple of nosy foreigners try to intrude in your life. But that is the thing, and I am afraid that I have to keep sounding like a broken record when I say that humans are ultimately social beings. We all crave to interact with other people, have refreshing conversations, and feel human touch, which is the bottom line, in my opinion.

I had a couple of similar experiences in Korea and Japan. For instance, when I was in Japan, a friend invited me over to his house. As we were touring his bedroom, he said, "My wife sleeps on the tatami mat on the floor and not on the bed." The way he spoke was so natural and nonchalant that it immediately made me laugh.

"What?" was the only response I could think of, and my friend simply nodded his head in response. At that instant, a thought flashed through my mind. I had been divorced several times, and every time I blamed myself for what went wrong in my marriages. Maybe, all I needed to do was be a bit rougher with my wives to make my marriages last. Obviously, my thought was nothing more than a joke. Here, what I'm trying to say is that once you put in enough effort into your relationships, people start trusting you and opening up to you; you come to discover seemingly unusual things that are a normal part of their lives.

Another time I was in Korea having a conversation with a dear friend, and he told me that the sea of Japan used to be a tidal lake. One could easily go from Korea to Japan, provided that the tide was in their favor. Once, the Korean king sent his daughter, Princess Nara, to an island called Henoko near the northeast region of Okinawa, Japan, to colonize it. There, Princess Nara proceeded to establish a tiny settlement, which is known as Nara, Japan today. That is where the eternal flame is located because it is said that the princess brought it there to establish what would come to be known as Japan. Even now, when you go to Nara, you can immediately notice two things. One is the sheer number of deer wandering around the streets, protected by anything that might harm them. Interestingly, the deers bow to tourists, a behavior they have learned over time to get food from the visitors. The second notable thing about the city is the eternal flame, which has continued to burn for centuries since its inception.

Years later, the Japanese invaded Korea, hoping to wipe it out of existence completely. They did not want the world to know that Japan had actually grown out of Korea, as that would have made people think that Koreans were the superior race since they had been around for much longer than the Japanese. As we were talking, I asked my friend where the term 'blue blood' came from. In response, he told me that when Genghis Khan came across and conquered Korea, they identified his descendants because they had a blue birthmark on one of their buttcheeks, which disappeared a month or so after the child's birth. Consequently, whenever a child of Korean descent was born with a blue birthmark, he was referred to as blue blood by the rest of the locals.

It is stories like these that continue to fascinate me. The sad part is you cannot learn this information from anywhere. No history books convey these kinds of myths and legends to the readers, and the only real way of getting to know them is by forming a connection with and talking to the locals. Frankly, traveling has always been a learning experience for me, which is why I continue to visit alien lands to get to know their people, culture, myths, and legends. As I write this, I cannot help but recall one of the poems of the Scottish poet, Robert Burns, which goes as follows,

Is there for honest poverty

That hings his head, an a' that?

The coward slave, we pass him by –

We dare be poor for a' that!

For a' that, an a' that,

Our toils obscure, an a' that,

The rank is but the guinea's stamp,

The man's the gowd for a' that.

What though on hamely fare we dine,

Wear hoddin grey, an a' that?

Gie fools their silks, and knaves their wine –

A man's a man for a' that.

For a' that, an a' that,

Their tinsel show, an a' that,

The honest man, tho e'er sae poor,

Is king o' men for a' that.

Ye see yon birkie ca'd 'a lord,'

Wha struts, an stares, an a' that?

Tho hundreds worship at his word,

He's but a cuif for a' that.

For a' that, an a' that,

His ribband, star, an a' that,

The man o' independent mind,

He looks an laughs at a' that.

A prince can mak a belted knight,

A marquis, duke, an a' that!

But an honest man's aboon his might –

Guid faith, he mauna fa' that!

For a' that, an a' that,

Their dignities, an a' that,

The pith o' sense an pride o' worth,

Are higher rank than a' that.

Then let us pray that come it may

(As come it will for a' that),

That Sense and Worth o'er a' the earth,

Shall bear the gree an a' that.

For a' that, an a' that,

It's coming yet for a' that,

That man to man, the world, o'er,

Shall brithers be for a' that.

~

Robert Burns

Burn's poem beautifully sketches out how people cannot be reduced to their wealth and worldly possessions. Perhaps, my favorite part of the poem is its end, where Burns paints the picture of a hopeful future for the reader, where men love each other, regardless of their differences. For me, that is what traveling is all about. Getting to know people, finding unity in diversity, and having enough kindness and empathy to relate to one another are all wonderful experiences. At the end of the day, we are all humans trying to comprehend our lives rationally.

Thoughts on Religion

The problem surfaces when one understands that life is a complex phenomenon that cannot be explained rationally. Its sheer unpredictability makes it incomprehensible. Think of it for a moment, would you? There must have been a time when you felt perfectly certain about your plans for the future.

You were positive that nothing could stop you from achieving the goals, milestones, and objectives you had set for yourself. It seemed like you were on a roll, checking off everything you planned to do to become successful. But then, an unforeseeable event threw you for a loop, and all of the progress you had made was for naught. In my case, I could have never predicted that four of my marriages would end in divorce. After all, my relationships started off great, and my partner and I put in a great deal of effort to make each other happy. Eventually, though, our bonds started fracturing due to reasons I could have never anticipated. Although distressing, the reality is that we have no control over our future, regardless of how meticulous and calculated our plans might be. At one point or another, we are confronted with occurrences that we could never have foretold, whether they be in the form of a loved one's death or finding out your partner is cheating on you. In that sense, it would be fair to say our entire lives are contingent on conditions and circumstances beyond our control. Regardless of our efforts, we simply cannot say that we have complete control over each and every aspect of our lives and that, my friends, is the bottom line.

Frankly, it can be pretty challenging to come to terms with such a dilemma. That is where religion comes in. The father of Sociology, Emile Durkheim, once said that religion imposes order on an otherwise chaotic world, and I cannot help but agree with such a point of view. See, belief in some sort of divine being is necessary for one to make sense of the nonsensical, isn't it? Otherwise, we would simply stop trying, thinking that if we do not control our lives, why bother putting in any effort? But such a point of view is nothing short of nihilism, which I am entirely against. Think of it this way, had I simply given up, would I have been able to make a life for myself in the States? Not at all. I would never have developed the entrepreneurial spirit that led me to become the chief executive officer and chairman of two public companies. In fact, I am confident that my entire existence would have devolved into chaos if I had adopted a nihilistic approach towards life.

As such, religion is something to be celebrated, in my opinion. Even if a person is not particularly religious, they must admit that religion dispels hope and optimism to an individual's life. In my case, I had several opportunities to simply stop trying. After all, I am deeply familiar with how it feels to lose a loved one. For instance, the pain of losing Daddy John ate me away from the inside, and I had to make a conscious effort to process my grief. I could have chosen to dwell in that void, letting darkness replace the vacuum left inside me after Daddy John's death. But there would have been no point in doing that. Instead, I chose to honor his legacy by carrying on his entrepreneurial wisdom and acumen. If religion helps people find the light as they are being enclosed by darkness, then there is no harm in that, not at all.

Nothing is worse than condemning someone for their religious belief. Whatever definition of God one might ascribe to, they are all the same in my view. Whether you are a Buddhist or a Christian, whether you believe in Allah or Bhagwan, all these labels are one and the same. They all point towards a divine being looking after its creation. In my opinion, religions clash against each other because of self-interested reasons. For instance, take the example of how the High Church of England was created. When the Pope repeatedly refused to annul Henry the VIII's marriage so he could remarry, he decided to split with the Pope and created the Church of England. He passed the Act of Succession and the Act of supremacy, according to which the King was the sole legal leader of the Church of England. Another interesting fact is that the reason the Pope decreed that the priests 'cannot marry' had nothing to do with the religious inscriptions of the Bible. Instead, the Pope wanted to ensure he did not have to share his taxes with the priests' families. And so, he devised a law stating that God does not want the priests to get married. I am not saying that is the way religion works today, not at all. Instead, I am just highlighting how it originated.

I was brought up in a religious household as a child, and I realized that religion could be incredibly dangerous. It has the potential to divide people into factions, and one needs to be diligent in using religious rhetoric. Back then, Roman Catholics never mixed with Protestants, and there was a palpable tension between the two groups. However, I could never bring myself to loathe someone just because of their religious beliefs. I could never accept such a hostile environment, not at any level, which is why I am respectful of all religions.

Frankly, looking at how religion evolved, you can see how all religious beliefs sprouted from the same idea. Every theological doctrine states the same thing: an innate, transcendent being put humans in the world. We just could not quite agree on the attributes and qualities of that God, the reason we were granted life, and what was going to happen to us. It did not take much long for factions of people to develop their own systems of faith, which were different from each other in some respects and similar in others. But once these differences were identified, religions started clashing amongst themselves, which led to several horrific wars such as the Eighty Years' War, the Crusades, and the Second World War. That is what humanity is all about, no? Instead of focusing on our similarities, we tend to focus on our differences. We are free to lead our lives the way we want to, so we can make our own choices. God gifted humanity intelligence, which is why each and every person thinks according to their own standards.

In my opinion, what matters is that we are humans at the end of the day. Even though our beliefs, values, morals, and ideals might differ from each other, we all share the same essence, which God granted to us. So, celebrate religion. Do not condemn others for celebrating religion in their way. Let them have that belief, as it might be the one thing keeping them sane in a world where it is pretty easy for one to get lost. Plus, what would be the point in hating a particular group of people over their religious beliefs? Doing so would only drive a wedge between you and them, which can have dire consequences for the rest of the world. Just take the example of the second world war, during which millions of Jews were subjected to the horrors of the concentration camps constructed by the Nazis. Approximately six million Jews died during WWI because of an individual's racist and xenophobic ideas. Can you imagine how significant that number was? Six million Jews were taken away from wives, sons, and daughters, only to be subjected to a horrific genocide because of a single person's fanaticism. Frankly, it makes one sick to think of the atrocities committed in WWII. Here, I want to issue a gentle plea to all of you. Never ever hate an individual for their religious identity. As long as their beliefs are not harming anyone, you should have no business criticizing them. Celebrate every identity because there is beauty in diversity.

In my case, I believe there is an innate being watching over us, whom most of humanity refers to as God. God put everyone on this Earth, whether they be good or bad. Every single one of us has a purpose, which is yet to be fulfilled. Sure, our purposes might vary from one another, but all of us were born with a particular mission. Once we have fulfilled our purpose, God calls us back. Whether or not there is an afterlife, we can never know for sure. Maybe, there is no afterlife, and God takes us away so that we can return to something else. All these are questions that will remain unanswered. I, for one, feel at peace, thinking that the man upstairs has granted my life a purpose. Otherwise, there would have been no meaning to my life. Personally, I still go to church, maybe not as often as I should, but I do go there. But if one goes to church for some peace and quiet, to be with their own people, and to gather their thoughts, can't one do all this anywhere?

Reflections on Death

I am content with the way my life has transpired, and I am happy knowing that I have a difference in the lives of the people around me, however shortlived or temporary it might be. Come to think of it, a lot of people are scared of death. But as someone nearing the end of his time, I can tell you one thing for sure: death is inevitable. Regardless of how rich or successful a person might be, they cannot escape death when it is out to collect your soul. However, one thing you can do is ensure that you leave a legacy behind. As I write this, I am reminded of a quote from the American novelist Ernest Hemingway, which reads along the following lines,

> *"Every man has two deaths when he is buried in the ground, and the last time someone says his name."*

Ernest Hemingway

Perhaps, instead of being afraid of death, we fear what will happen to our memory once we bid farewell to the world. Would anyone remember us? Would our families remember us fondly, or would we remind them of a cruel, selfish person? Would anyone even pray for us? All these questions nag us whenever we are forced to think about death. But, if you look closely, you will realize that these thoughts have a common theme: none of them is related to our worldly possessions. Think about it for a minute. I am sure that most of you have been to a funeral during your lifetime. Did you ever hear someone at a funeral saying, "It is a shame so, and so lost his life. They were so rich." After your death, nobody remembers you for your flashy cars, massive mansions, or the money sitting idly in your accounts. What people do remember you for is the difference you made in their lives.

Mark my words, the best way to leave a legacy behind is to be kind to the people around you. A person may not remember you for your worldly gains, but they will always think back to when you were there for them in their time of need. That is the philosophy I have adopted in my life. As a seventy-four-year-old man, the one thing I can say for sure is that humans are nothing if not social animals. We need each other, and none of us can survive in complete isolation. As such, I do my best to be kind, compassionate, and empathetic to my family, my employees, my friends, and everyone else in between, and I hope you are following a similar kind of approach in life.

See, once you reach a certain age, the prospect of dying someday suddenly becomes more realistic to you. When you are a child, death does not rattle you the same way it rattles people slightly older than you. Sure, you might be acutely aware of the fact that death represents the conclusion of an individual's life, but that belief does not get to your head. Only after one has reached a certain age and witnessed the death of their loved ones, they realize that they, too, will suffer the same fate sometime in the future.

In my experience, death is not something to be feared. It is just a part of our lives, which we cannot escape at any cost. So, what is the point in feeling apprehensive about one's ultimate fate? Think about it for a minute. From my experience, the more a person is scared about death, the less they manage to get something out of their lives. If the fear of death cripples one to the point that it is the only thing they can think about, they will not live their lives to the fullest.

In my view, happiness resides in those fleeting moments of our life, where we do not feel burdened by any worries, anxieties, or fears. If that is true, how can someone constantly worried about death enjoy those moments of happiness? The bottom line is they cannot, so it is better to make peace with the fact that the grim reaper will come for our soul one day, and there is absolutely nothing we can do to avoid such a fate.

In my experience, those who have seen many deaths in their lives are the most empathetic of all people. They understand how short our lives truly are, and as such, they try to make the most of whatever hand they were dealt at the time of their birth. It might sound peculiar, but there is a certain beauty in death. If all of humanity was immortal and no one ever died, would we actually appreciate each other? I do not think so. It is only because of the concept of death that we realize what it means to lose a loved one, and as such, we cherish each other, knowing fully well that our lives might come to an end at any second. In fact, it is because of this exact belief that I do not want my death to be a sad occasion.

In my view, death should not represent an opportunity to mourn the deceased. It is not like crying over a person's death is going to bring them back. However sad that might sound, that is just the nature of the world we inhabit. People die, period. Here, I cannot help but be reminded of a quote from the novel, The Catcher in the Rye. Holden Caulfield, the protagonist of the novel, says,

"When you're dead, they really fix you up. I hope to hell when I do die; somebody has sense enough to just dump me in the river or something. Anything except sticking me in a goddamn cemetery. People coming and putting a bunch of flowers on your stomach on Sunday, and all that crap. Who wants flowers when you're dead? Nobody."

Holden Caulfield, The Catcher in the Rye

It's true, no? Who wants flowers after dying? At least, I do not wish for my grave to be adorned with wreaths and heirlooms after my death. Those artifacts would be of no use to me in the afterlife now, would they? I would much rather prefer to be cherished while I am still alive, and I am sure most people feel the same way. Sadly, the world we inhabit is not structured to function that way. Almost every person is sacked with responsibilities, and it is rare for someone to take the time to appreciate their loved ones, which, frankly, is quite disheartening.

In my opinion, friends and family should always come first. Life is ephemeral, and we might be dead today, tomorrow, or after ten or more years. No being on this planet can defy death, so keep your loved ones close to you. Cherish them while they are still alive. That way, you would not feel miserable once they bid farewell to the world. Maybe, that is why I do not want my funeral to be a sad occasion. I do not want people to guilt-trip themselves for not spending more time with me. I am positive that when I finally do die, I will not have any grudges against anyone. Just like there is no point in decorating one's grave with flowers, it is quite futile to resent someone in the afterlife. Plus, who is to say that I would even possess a consciousness after my death? I certainly wish I do, but then again, these are questions whose answer will always remain unknown.

For some unknown reason, Caulfield's words resonate with my perception of death. I, for one, do not want my death to be a grievous occasion. Instead, the one thing I do wish for is that my funeral is nothing short of a party. I want everyone at my funeral to get drunk while a New Orleans Jazzband plays music at one corner of the cemetery. I wish to hear the sound of my loved ones laughing as I am being lowered into my final resting place. Even if I am physically not present there, I want the mood at my wake to be cheery and not melancholic or pitiful.

Perhaps, my biggest wish is that nobody at my funeral remembers me as a selfish or self-absorbed person. Nothing would dishearten me more than people thinking of me as a person devoid of any admirable traits and qualities. I want the people at my funeral to smile and laugh as they reminisce over their memories of me. As long as my loved ones celebrate my legacy, it does not matter when and how I die. In fact, I would be perfectly content and at peace.

CHAPTER 10:

NO PLACE FOR TOXICITY

Marriage is a sacred union of a man and a woman – usually – one that is regulated by laws, customs, and rules when two people decide to come together. The universal nature of marriage within different cultures and societies depends on many social and personal attributes that help form its structure, such as emotional and sexual gratification, division of labor between man and wife, along with the satisfaction of personal needs for companionship and affection. Its contemporary function, and perhaps its historical purpose, is procreation, looking after young ones, their education, civilization, and socialization.

When two people get married, they make a vow that they will stick together forever, through thick and thin, and make it work. They plan their lives around each other and have kids that they look up to. They work to raise well-behaved, good humans so they may take the world as they go further. They have dreams and plans of living a good life and that as long as they have each other, they will be okay.

The way I see it, marriage is an empty box given to the couple at the time of marriage. The commitment these two people hold toward each other will drive them to fill this container with what they need. When two people love and respect each other, they also box these values to use and reuse further into the marriage. As they keep learning about each other and growing, the box keeps getting bigger and fuller. It never goes away, though. It always stays with these people for as long as they stick together. As the couple evolves, so does the nature of their duties. From nursing and nurturing little humans to guiding adults, this couple takes on all sorts of challenges. Sometimes, these people make it through, while other times. Couples go their own way when the marriage does not work. Some have the courage to keep going, while others take their half of the box and store it away forever.

As adults, we realize how much is out of our control as we grow up. And honestly, we do not control much. We might have all the sales forecast charts in front of us when we launch a product or devise a strategy, but there is no guarantee that things will turn out exactly that way. Similarly, in our personal lives too, we do not know what will happen next. For instance, I went through multiple divorces before finding my one true love, lost two children in their adulthood, and went through various business ventures and experiences before I got to where I am today. As long as we keep going with an open mind, we will get to where we want. No matter what you do in life, you have to be persistent to get to where you want. To be with the person you love, you need to keep putting in the effort every single day, or else your relationship will start cracking.

There are quite a few reasons marriages fail. Over the years, divorce rates have soared, while couples counseling is more common now than before. Statistics really make you think about what is happening behind the scenes, but experts have managed to make a list of reasons why marriages are failing at such colossal rates. It is not just sad that this is happening on such a large scale, but many professions see the break up of marriage as a way of conducting business, often putting in minimal effort to save the marriage. Regardless, divorce, especially when kids are involved, gets intense and often too heavy to process because of the number of people involved in the process. Couples must try their best to make their relationships work, and if things still do not flesh out the way they want, the best option is to part ways but still maintain a healthy relationship for the sake of their own mental health and that of their children's.

Some reasons that marriages break up include:

1. Little or no investment

When either of the two counterparts starts lacking in terms of how much time and effort is put into the relationship, eventually, the other person will start to slow down as well. You see, two people are needed to make the relationship work, and while holding the forte can work in turns, the husband and wife must both do their part to keep going. Just like a job in the corporate world, even marriage needs training, skills, and hard work to keep going. The only difference is that you get paid in comfort, love, and understanding.

When people feel that their relationship is falling apart, it is best to sit down and talk about what is bothering them. A communication gap can be deathly because once things are left unsaid, they have a habit of drilling holes into a relationship. If couples feel that they cannot figure out the problem together, professional help is always available.

2. Lack of communication

In my opinion, the day couples stop talking to each other is the day they set themselves up for failure. Marriage requires decisions to be made on a daily basis, from cumulative chores to individual responsibilities. However, when a married couple stops talking to each other, there will come a time when each of them has a problem with the way things are done, not simply because of the task but also because they will begin to lose sight of the person they used to be with their spouse around. As sad as it sounds, a small gap in communication is as lethal to marriage as a drop of cyanide is to human life. Long-term decisions include what each spouse wants to do with their career, which spouse will be dedicating more time to the kids, and other such concerns that require teamwork to move forward. Additionally, couples need to take time out every day to check in with each other and discuss what is bothering them; maybe even go out together to get out of their busy lives. When problems are constantly brushed down, one or both parties may feel ignored and taken for granted, eventually causing the relationship to fall apart.

Marriage is a relationship that needs work every single day. Some days you will feel like doing more, while on other days, you may do less, which is fine as long as you let your spouse know how you are feeling. Just like your love-hate relationship with your job, where you have to inform your supervisor of the decisions, for instance, not going to work because of illness, et cetera, your spouse also needs to know that you are feeling sub-par any specific day. As long as you bring your partner on board, the two of you should be able to figure things out together.

3. Financial issues

Another one of the biggest reasons for the fall of marital relationships is insufficient financial standing. If one spouse earns while the other is taking care of the kids, they might likely start feeling like the other person is not doing enough. The earning individual may feel like the at-home parent is not doing enough, while the spouse who has given up their career for children might feel like they are being taken for granted.

Sometimes, couples find themselves struggling even after they both put in work to earn the financial means to move forward. An addiction one spouse possesses or the inability to handle financial matters by the other may lead to couples ending their relationship as well. At the end of the day, it is always useful to speak about who will be doing what in marriage before two people tie the knot. Unsaid expectations can be a huge factor that causes marriages to come to an end.

4. Lack of intimacy and sex

According to experts, a majority of divorces happen when couples lose intimate touch with each other. Whether it be emotional or physical, intimacy is one of the key aspects in making relationships flourish. Sexual intercourse is much more than a surface-level act. It is a sign of trust and respect between spouses and an important type of marital connection. It is often women who are the first ones to seek out therapy to fix their relationship. Men usually have a much higher libido than women, and this is often seen as a problem between couples, causing a rift or discrepancy between them.

While some problems can be solved through mere communication, reviving intimacy in a relationship is usually a little more complex. Many times, the spark between the couple dies down, while the romance diminishes as the couple progresses through their marriage. The fire simply stops burning, and couples decide to call the marriage off, sometimes even if all other aspects of the relationship are working seemingly fine.

5. Familial or societal pressure

Our families express their thoughts on who we should or should not marry. Women tend to be chasing their biological clock, and men, too, feel the societal pressure of getting married and settling down. The rush may cause them to pick partners out of making others happy, putting themselves second in the process. When you make a lifelong decision based on emotions rather than rationality, the chances of divorce automatically spike in such circumstances.

The problem worsens when kids are involved in the process. When couples do not take a stand for each other or the marriage as a whole, the kids end up confused in the process because they do not understand what is going on. Many years down the line, couples understand that rushing into a relationship they were not at all ready for was probably the biggest mistake in their lives, but by that time, it is already too late to do anything but divorce your partner. In such situations, getting a divorce is better because things may get out of hand. However, as the old saying goes, prevention is better than cure; hence, making a wise decision at the start is better than regretting it later.

6. Lack of self-knowledge

When people do not know what they want, or rather who they want, they end up in bad marriages where their spouse is either chosen by their family or due to external circumstances that are not thought through. In some families, people marry those that look good with them on paper or for some sort of a deal. Sometimes, marriage is also used as a sham to get what one particular individual is after, and once their purpose is fulfilled, they decide to terminate the relationship. The most important part of it all is to realize what you want and what works for you. Meet new people, discover your feelings and emotions, and know the type of person you want to spend your life with. Document how certain situations and people make you feel. Things that make you uncomfortable or unconfident need to go out the window, while those that match your vibe are something you should pursue. Whether you are twenty-five or thirty, remember that you need to know what works for you to move ahead in life. Otherwise, you will catch yourself going round and round in circles, trying to figure out what works for you.

My first marriage was while I was still in Scotland. I had two kids out of that marriage who stayed with their mother, my ex-wife, Patricia. I decided to end that marriage because as I explored the world, I got to learn so many things I had never known before. My second marriage was to my ex-wife Linda, who also gave me two kids. Although that marriage ended because Linda cheated on me, I love my kids dearly to this day. One of the kids, my son Adrian, was out of that marriage, and he was murdered. I will talk about it in the later chapter. My daughter is still alive and is a mother to three beautiful kids, who are almost as angelic as she is. She is an amazing, strong woman, and I share a strong bond with her. She reminds me a lot of her mother, who is a strong, resilient woman, not afraid of any challenge she is put through. My third marriage was a happenstance because my ex-wife had gotten pregnant before we were even married. All I knew at that point was that I wanted the child to be born a legitimate one and not an illegitimate one. That marriage lasted just about two years and died down much too soon after I found out that I was being cheated on, yet again. After I got divorced for the third time, I moved to San Diego with my now ten-year-old son, where I hired someone from abroad to take care of him. I fell in love with this young lady quite soon, and we ended up married for a good twelve years. We had two boys, and we raised them well.

I have had quite a good relationship with all my exes through the years. Most of them were for the sake of my children, but through all my relationships, I would say I had exes who understood that we did not work because not all marriages are supposed to last over. There was no animosity between us as we went through life and grew apart as individuals. Every time one of my relationships ended, I was convinced that marriage was not for me. In fact, after my fourth marriage, I was mentally convinced that all I was going to do was date women and have short-term relationships because I had given my best each time to no avail.

The pattern in my marriages was the same. We would get married out of love, have a few kids, realize the love was gone, I would get cheated on, and then we would split. Or so I thought. I would get so upset every time I ended up single; I would focus on my work. I would work day and night, trying to make things work without realizing the actual problem. It was not until I started to reflect on my actions and on myself as a whole that I realized what was wrong. And honestly, Sandy helped me see many things much clearer. Hence, I came to write this book to help everyone out there.

Not too long ago, I realized that marriage is like riding a bike. Sometimes you have help to get through the track in front of you, while other times, you need to pick yourself up and get back on your vehicle and keep going. There are only pauses, falls, and elevations on the way, but no stopping or backing down unless you want to end the relationship. When my marriages ended one after the other, I was blinded. I never saw that I was also part of the problem. Naturally, if the lesson keeps repeating for you, you must know that the universe is at work to make you learn something you cannot pick up. It took me four divorces to understand that I had been treating my relationships like my work because that is all I had ever known. I got too busy building my empire(s), ignored my spouses and children, delved too hard into my board meetings to realize that I needed to be an active member in their lives for the relationship to work. At the back of my head, I had decided that just because I was earning for the family, I was fulfilling my responsibilities. However, I never realized that human connection could never be replaced. And as I grew into my age, year after year, I slowly started bringing my workplace practices home. It is funny, isn't it? Sometimes the answers are right in front of us, yet we take so long to understand the solution. In fact, most of the time, the solution lies within us or around us, and even then, we struggle to comprehend its simplicity. We are used to doing things the difficult way too often to realize that sometimes the answer is quite simple. In my case, it was sharing more responsibility as a father and a husband, and the multiple split-ups were the clear symptoms of the problem. I was blind-sided by wanting to move forward every time I gained success. I needed to learn how to be a family man that I hope

I now know, but it took me a while to understand something so unpretentious.

Life is a journey, and you are on a bus. You have to keep getting off at stops that will take you further in life. Sometimes you have to wait longer for the next bus to come along, while other times, you might even miss it because you were late, but that is okay because another bus is coming and you just have to brace yourself to get on it. My understanding of the world is that it is an oyster. You have to keep your head high and move forward, grab the opportunities you get and do your best. Sometimes you will be grasping at straws, while other times, you will be in a pit of gold coins when everything is going your way, but this is when you have to remember to be humble. Stay human and stay connected to other beings.

No matter what happens today, tomorrow is a new day. The sun will rise from the east and set in the west, and it is going to be sunny and then dark. You have countless moments at your disposal to do the one thing you have been dying to do. It is possible and doable. The answer is buried under your own efforts. All you have to do is fly endlessly till you get there. No one can do anything for you if you are not willing. When the positive surrounds you, be grateful and share the happiness and good times. And when you are taken over by the negative, stay grounded and understand where your shortcoming lies. That is the only way to move forward without getting way over your head and also ensuring that your sense of self-worth does not go underground. It is doable; all you need to do is keep trying till you get it.

Be a Better Spouse

Many couples out there manage to save themselves from divorce by getting proper help. When you reach out and make amends in your relationship, as soon as things get out of control, there is a higher chance of salvaging your marriage. There are a few things couples can do to stay with each other, especially in the face of a difficult patch in their marriage. It is crucial to understand that there is no way around a concrete solution, and you have to take the challenge head-on if you want to stay together. A few things I have picked out of my failed marriages have been listed below as someone who wants to help others out of the rut I was stuck in.

1. Your marriage needs attention

Couples need to understand that you need to pay as much attention to each other as you do to your hobbies. People who spend considerable time and effort on themselves have shown to stay together for longer periods of time. When married people take time out for each other, they get more time to communicate with each other, giving them a chance to get more problems out in the open. Sometimes, people throw up their hands and give in to difficulties instead of understanding that a stronger relationship lies on the other side of their hurdle. Makes sense, does it not? For couples beginning to experience issues, it is advised that they read books on marriage, try different methods of conflict resolution, practice various communication techniques, and reach out to professional help to fix their marriage. Get together with your spouse and read up together, helping each other learn and resolve issues together.

2. Prioritize your spouse

You should treat your spouse as a priority, ensuring your attitude with them is better than with anyone else. When people live together, they tend to treat each other worse than they treat strangers. There is no doubt that familiarity breeds contempt, but for a marriage to work, couples must work to ensure that only the opposite is true. Setting boundaries for yourself and your spouse at the start of the marriage is essential to respect each other and treat your spouse with integrity. Remember, you get what you give, so do not expect what you do not give.

3. Support your spouse

Encourage your partner and support them to achieve their dreams and goals. To make a marriage successful, the two people must work as if in a partnership, happy for each other's success. Good spouses hold the forte when their partner needs time for themselves to achieve their goals and dreams. Sometimes it can get scary to pursue something on your own. Hence, you should be the partner your spouse needs to be there for them.

4. Do activities together

Pick up activities that help you spend more time together. It could just be a short walk after family dinner on Friday or a lunch plan during the week. Anything that will take you both out of your regular routine will do you good as you get to spend time with each other. Use this time to communicate, maybe talk about the best part of each other's day or a simple catch-up with what each of you did through the day. It is not all about having a full-fledged vacation for yourself. Sometimes, it is the little moments you need to get through the day with your spouse.

5. The grass is not always greener on the other side

It is true. Most people leave their current relationships only to find someone else with similar problems, if not the same ones. It is easy to think that other people have it better than you when you are caught up in your own problems, hence the emphasis on solving your problems before they get too big. Often, people regret leaving their current relationships and not working on them when they had the chance. Once a good thing is gone, it is nearly impossible to get it back. Hence, unless you are absolutely sure about what you want, gauge your options carefully to avoid any regretful decisions.

6. Let little things slide

You cannot always get mad at your spouse at every little squabble you have. When you live with people for a long time, the best strategy to stick together is to pick your battles. Some days you will make a mistake that you will need to let go of, and other days you will be the one who will have to forgive the other. Either way, you have to remember that your companionship works on trust, compromise, and, most importantly, respect. Understanding that your spouse is also human and is allowed to slack off sometimes will help you understand your situation better, helping the two of you go easy on each other. Appreciating and acknowledging your spouse leads to them reciprocating the same, making the relationship flourish on its own. The most important thing you can do for your partner is to make them feel like they are not invisible. Appreciate your spouse, treat them with kindness and respect, trust them, and see the relationship flourish.

7. Never let the friendship go

To be good at any partnership, you need to establish friendly boundaries first. The reason for this connection is that above all else, you need to hear each other out as friends to get by. You can play house in certain roles such as parenting, cooking for the children, taking them to school, but at the end of the day, you are also your own person who needs a friend to listen to their woes. Establishing a friendly relationship at the start of your marriage will help the both of you remember that you are more than two people tied in a marital bond. Everything else comes after you have created a boundary of respect and care for each other.

8. Be faithful

One of the biggest aspects of any relationship is your fidelity and the integrity you have for your partner. Once you are committed to one person, you have to take ownership of the bond, understanding that both of you are in it for the long run. External affairs and seeking someone else out destroy a relationship like parasites infest a crop site. And the only way to get rid of the parasitic damage is to cut it off at the knees, so it has no chance of coming back. According to experts, once you cheat on your spouse and they find out, the nature of your relationship will change forever no matter what you do. Couples who indulge in such activities often develop toxic traits that slowly become stronger as they move forward. If you want to end the relationship because you want to give someone else a chance, do it the right way. Respect lies far beyond having love for someone. While it is normal to fall out of love with someone because love is an emotion that fluctuates, respect and trust make up part of your belief system. You may find love again, but the forgiveness will take time to come by. Wilful forgiveness is difficult, and no one is worth losing over infidelity. You may never be able to fix what you have done but you can hope to be forgiven by asking for forgiveness. You can try and seek guidance for what you have done to ensure that you do not repeat your bad habits again. To err is to human, to forget should not happen, but to forgive is strength. We all make mistakes, some intentionally and some by accident. As the Bible says, "He that is without sin among you, let him first cast a stone at her." Mistakes and sins are part of life. Neither the giver nor the receiver forgets them but learn from them. The biggest challenge becomes to forgive those who have wronged you.

*"Forgive others not because they deserve forgiveness
but because you deserve peace."*

9. Do not complain about your spouse

Unless you are seeking advice on how to be a better partner, do not complain to your friends or other family members about what your spouse is like at their weakest. We are all human beings trying to get by in life. The best thing you can do to help your partner get out of bad or toxic habits is to seek professional help.

When you understand that you are only a human being, and so is your partner, it will be easier for you to understand their mistakes and vice versa. But talking to someone else about intimate matters only gives them a chance to interfere in your relationship, which is not a smart move at all, to begin with. Unless it is somebody who you deeply trust and know will not come between your relationship, you need to set a boundary even with your family before saying something that may hurt your spouse. Remember, they are already going through a tough time, and imposing a difficult situation on them might bring about consequences you are not ready for. When you are in a relationship, you need to think about the other person as well as the two of you now working as a unit.

10. Appreciate and acknowledge each other

When you make the other person's marital contributions feel valued, they will do much more than they are expected. Marriages often begin falling apart when you walk by each other without even blinking and fail at the feet of treating your spouse as if they are invisible. When people become indifferent, it does not matter what you do for them; it is all going to go unnoticed and unappreciated. Unfortunately, this desensitization is highly likely in a marriage as well.

Speaking from my experience, you need to balance your responsibilities. You are operating in many social and public spheres, such as being a friend, a professional, a neighbor, and so much more that it is easy to forgive your identity in the private sphere. People who manage all their roles subtly get by in life much more easily because they never lose sight of who they are. I admit to this day that a part of the reason my wives found attention from other men is that I was too busy working day in and out to notice either of them.

*"The great marriages are partnerships. It can't be
a great marriage without being a partnership."*

Helen Mirren

CHAPTER 11:

NEVER A GOODBYE

"I cannot say, and I will not say

That he is dead. He is just away.

With a cheery smile and a wave of the hand,

He has wandered into an unknown land,

And left us dreaming how very fair,

It needs must be since he lingers there.

And you – oh you, who the wildest yearn

For an old-time step, and the glad return,

Think of him faring on, as dear

In the love of there as the love of here,

Think of him still as the same. I say,

He is not dead – he is just away."

~

James Whitcomb Riley

See, the death of a loved one drastically alters your approach in life. Your entire perspective, how you perceive the world, and even your core values, beliefs, and ideals undergo a fundamental shift, leaving you high and dry. Losing someone close to you is nothing short of a liminal event, and it completely redefines your personality. For most people, death means the end of an individual's life, but such a definition is quite restrictive, don't you think? It completely forgoes the kind of toll death can have on the loved ones of the deceased, how it fractures their entire existence into a million little pieces, and how difficult it is to go back to the normal course of life after a loved one's death.

But as someone whose time is running out, I can say one thing without a sliver of doubt. Death is a part of life, and no matter how hard you try, you cannot save anyone from the relentless clutches of the grim reaper. The most you can do is try and preserve their legacy. It might seem peculiar, but I truly believe all of us are a culmination of the people we have encountered in our lives, be it your friends, family, or partner.

For instance, take the example of a child. When a baby is born, they inherit the traits, characteristics, and qualities of their parents. That makes sense, no? After all, if someone lives half of their lives with their parents, it is natural for them to mimic the latter's behaviorisms, demeanors, and attitudes. But when an individual's parents finally bid farewell to the world, it is not like they simply stop existing, no. Instead, they continue to live on through their children, which is how their legacy is preserved.

I, for one, believe this fact to be true for every relationship. When a father or a mother loses their child, it is a traumatizing experience, to say the least, and healing from that trauma can be a lifelong project. The point I am trying to make, however, is that the departed are not always gone. Instead, the essence of their spirit is perpetually manifested in the mannerisms, behaviorisms, and attitudes of their loved ones, as is the case when a parent loses a child. Sure, it might not be very explicit. It can be downright subtle, but that does not change how the dead continue to persist in the world. I refuse to believe the day a person dies, their entire existence simply disappears. It cannot be that simple, considering how complex and multifaceted the world is.

Like I mentioned earlier in the book, I became a single father when Adrian was only four. Frankly, it was challenging to look after a child without having the support of a spouse. Still, I managed to fulfill my responsibilities as a father while staying on top of my work. Sure, there were times where I faltered, but that is only natural, especially for a first-time father. Now when I reflect on it, it must have been much more difficult for Adrian as he never had a constant mother figure in his life. See, a mother's love and affection are crucial for developing a child's cognitive, emotional, and psychological faculties. It is rather sad that my son never got to experience a mother's love fully. After all, the purity, innocence, and sincerity of a child's relationship with their mother are otherworldly.

Essentially, I had to serve as both Adrian's mother and father. After my ex-wife and I separated, she vanished from Adrian's life, and it took her three or four years to reappear. As such, my son could never form a strong bond with his mother, which I wish would not have happened. But we cannot control every aspect of our lives, and it is futile to lament the past. To be honest, Adrian never cared much about meeting his mother, but it was a pressing issue to me. In fact, I was the one who kept telling him he needed to go and visit his mother. It was only because of insistence that he agreed to patch his relationship with his mom.

Earlier, I described that when my ex-wife and I divorced, she told me Victoria was not my child, implying that her biological father was someone else and that she had cheated on me. Well, after I remarried, my then-wife asked me why I chose to believe her? She compelled me to think of all the other instances where Victoria and Adrian's mother told me things that were not true in reality. What if she had intentionally lied to me to become Victoria's sole custodian? Frankly, I barely slept that night and deliberated on that question.

It took me a while to realize my then-wife was right, and I decided to go back to the courts. There, I requested the adjudicators to force my ex-wife into taking a paternity test. Come to think of it, that entire ordeal was quite amusing. Usually, it is the woman trying to prove the man is, in fact, the biological father of her child. But there I was, making my ex-wife undergo a paternity test to prove that Victoria was indeed my biological child.

Ultimately, the courts ruled that Victoria was undeniably my child. Looking back, there were two main reasons why I chose to test my daughter's ancestry. First and foremost, I asked myself why I should choose to believe someone who has repeatedly lied to me. One might think of me as too much of a skeptic, but the fact of the matter is circumstances can change people. I do not think people are innately evil and cruel. It is just that when we are pinned against the walls, sometimes our only option to save our skin is to opt for a rather unethical course of action. I am sure my ex-wife did not lie just to spite me, but because her circumstances came to define her actions. All these facts constituted one of the reasons why I chose to make her undergo a paternity test.

Secondly, if I had simply chosen to believe that Victoria was not my kid, there was a possibility that I would have never put in the effort to develop a healthy and mutually reinforcing relationship with her. Had that been the case, what would have I done if she one day revealed I was our daughter's real father? What if she one day came to me and asked why I refused to take action to prove Victoria was my child? Even thinking about such a possibility kills me. Worst of all, the thought of Victoria growing up and taking her father as an irresponsible and careless person compelled me to take the paternity test. All these questions nagged the back of my mind, and I realized that a paternity test was the only viable option if I wanted to retain my sanity.

I needed to get a clear understanding of what was true and untrue, which is why I decided to go back to the courts. If it turned out that Victoria was my biological child, so be it. I promised myself to stand up, assume responsibility, and be the best father I could be to my daughter. That has been one of my core purposes in life, and only God and my children know whether or not I have succeeded in doing so.

Raising Adrian as a single parent was an incredibly challenging task, as it should have been. I had a job, so I needed to clock in every day for work. When he learned how to walk, things became even more difficult. See, children are naturally inquisitive, and they tend to gravitate towards seemingly mundane objects. But their beautiful little brains cannot wrap around the idea that these objects might pose a danger to them. How often do you see a child trying to pick an object double their weight, only for it to drop right on top of their head? Obviously, I could not expect him to fend for himself while I was handling business. That would have been incredibly unethical, and it angers me how common it is for parents to leave their toddlers all alone.

It was not long before I realized the need to arrange someone to look after Adrian while I was engrossed in work. In the beginning, I could not think of anyone responsible enough to take care of my son, but that was just my fatherliness expressing itself. However, as I mentioned earlier, the niece of one of my former colleagues was trying to find a job abroad, and the timing could not have been better. Her name was Christine, and she was an ambitious young lady. Over time, she settled into her job well, giving me the time to care for my own needs. Whereas previously, I could barely make the time to look after myself, things became easier after Christine joined.

But both of us knew that eventually, our little arrangement would come to an end, and that was exactly what happened. After Christine left, though, I met my fourth wife shortly afterward, and she became a nanny of sorts for Adrian. As time progressed, we decided to get married and had two children of our own. We were in San Diego at the time, and I distinctly recall a memory from our days there. When my family and I shifted to America's finest city, we had to live in a hotel temporarily or, at least, until I could put a down payment on a home. Those were the good old days, and I remember feeling both joy and sadness seeing Adrian grow up into a handsome young man.

See, Adrian had decided to join the school band, and saxophone became his instrument of choice. Whenever I would return to the hotel room after a long day at work, I would find Adrian feeling down. Basically, he could not practice playing the saxophone in the hotel room because the other guests would complain. Frankly, it made sense. He was still learning the instrument, and anyone who has heard a saxophone knows how blaring of a sound it produces when played by a newbie. Eventually, though, he started going to the bottom of the car park and behind the trashcans to practice his instrument.

Frankly, that was a heartbreaking experience for me, and I asked myself, 'God, what have I done to this kid.' Adrian deserved to live in a home where he could do whatever he wanted without any fear. Instead, he was stuck in a car park, and no one there showed any real appreciation for his talents. But I soon realized that I, too, never had support during my childhood. I never had a place to go and practice, but I grew up to be more than okay. So, I told myself there was no point in thinking of myself as a bad father who could not support his child's ambitions.

As a father, you always wish to give your children all those luxuries and comforts that you never got to experience in your childhood. Sometimes, however, circumstances restrict you from providing your child with everything they deserve, and when that happens, you cannot help but feel like a bad parent. The same happened to me when I watched Adrian practicing the saxophone next to some garbage bins in a car park. I felt miserable, and there was nothing I could do except thinking that I was not fit for the role of being a father in my son's life.

Thankfully, however, I did not let my thoughts mediate my actions, and it was not long before a thought crossed my mind. See, there are times when things do not turn out the way you expect them to, which was exactly what Adrian must have realized, knowing that he could not play the saxophone in the hotel room. In my opinion, such an experience is important for children, as it helps in keeping them grounded and humble. Instead of taking things for granted, they try to find happiness in the littlest of things and believe me, that is all you need sometimes.

Looking back at it, playing the saxophone while standing next to smelly disgusting-looking garbage bins must have given Adrian an important life lesson. It taught him there were no shortcuts in life, and if you really wanted to pursue something, you needed to get out of your comfort zone and find a way of working on your interests legally and correctly. That experience turned out to be one of those moments where you do not know whether to feel happy or sad. I felt sad because the entire ordeal made me think I was not doing enough for my child, and I felt happy knowing that Adrian was breaking out of his comfort zone at a relatively young age. Watching that four-year-old evolve into an intelligent man comprised some of the most rewarding and frustrating moments of my life.

However, it goes without saying that I loved Adrian with my entire heart. Sure, there were times when we did not see eye to eye on certain topics, but that did not change the fact that he was my blood. He gifted me one of the most amazing experiences of my life, that of fatherhood. Adrian was my third child, and as such, he taught me the ins and outs of being a father. After him, I was blessed with several other children, and I could not be more proud of any of them. It is rather scary, no, how quickly time slips through our fingers? It seems like only yesterday. I was trying to assume the responsibility that is part and parcel of fatherhood. But now, even my youngest daughter, Victoria, has three kids. Not only is she a dedicated mother, but she is also playing a very important role in one of my companies. Because of my age, I am not involved in their lives as much as I should be, but I do try my best to check up on them from time to time. I guess the point I am trying to make is I could not have been a good father to my other children had it not been for Adrian, who taught me everything I know about fatherhood.

Perhaps, that is why losing him plunged me into a spiral of grief and guilt, and it took me all of my strength to come to terms with his death.

The Cruel Clutch of Death

Like I mentioned earlier, people are not innately bad. Instead, it is their circumstances that entice them into making poor decisions. When Adrian got hooked on drugs, that was one of those moments where I felt like I had failed as a father. After Adrian was discharged from the army, he started using narcotics. Perhaps, the things he experienced while he was on tour were too much for him to bear. Maybe, the intoxicating effects of drugs were all he needed to come to terms with the cruelty and wickedness he got to witness with his very own eyes. These are all questions, the answers of whom cannot be more than mere speculations.

When I discovered that Adrian was hooked on opiates, I tried my best to send him to rehabilitation centers, where he could get clean. I told him that he could no longer visit my home until he sobered up. As much as it hurt me seeing my son high on drugs and not even knowing who he was at times, there was nothing I could do to prevent him from succumbing to his addictions. To be honest, watching your child slowly wither away is one of the worst spectator sports, and it pained me to my core knowing that Adrian was slowly dying from his addictions. But I could not walk away. Think of it for a second. How could I have simply left him to his own devices?

I did not want to be the type of father who could not even acknowledge that his child was a drug addict. That is just not who I am as a human being. I tried my best to support him and guide him throughout this ordeal. I spent countless hours trying to make him understand that if he continued to dabble in narcotics, it would not be long before his life crashed and burned. Maybe, I was a bit harsh at times, but you have to understand that dealing with a drug-addict child is not as easy as it seems. It eats you up from the inside, seeing your own blood gradually rot away. Regardless, there is one thing I can say for sure. All the tough calls I had to make were done keeping Adrian's best interests in mind. Unfortunately, though, all of my efforts were in vain.

When I heard about Adrian's death, I began to bawl. See, losing a child is, perhaps, the most painful thing one can experience, and I would not wish it on the worst of my enemies. A piece of my soul was ripped away, and there was nothing, absolutely nothing I could do to replace the void left behind. They say the first thing you forget after a loved one's death is their voice, but that is not true for me. To this day, I can distinctly recall the way Adrian looked, all of his behaviors, mannerisms, and demeanors, the way he laughed, and I can never forget any of those things.

But Adrian's death was not the only thing to rattle me to the core. My other son, Cannon, fell victim to narcotics and passed away shortly after Adrian's death, succumbing once more to drugs. I often get angry that two of my boys were taken away from me. Adrian at the age of thirty-four, and Cannon at the young age of twenty-six. However, I often reflect and realize that these boys had travelled this world and seen so much of it; more than most of us do in a lifetime.

Adrian, an all CIF football player, was at war in Iraq and was honorably discharged as a highly decorated army veteran. He was a man of integrity, character, and honor. He kept to himself, and often, I would ask him to tell me what he was going through so I could step in and help him. He always refused, telling me that his family was too important to be exposed. The people he got involved with were bad, and he put his family's safety first, regardless of his circumstances.

Cannon, the thoughtful one, had a kind smile and readily helped those that were battling addiction for many years. My family has even started a foundation to help others that may be dealing with such problems. We go under the domain www. brothersforeverfoundation.com, where you can learn more about my wonderful boys.

Even today, my stepdaughter battles with drugs, but I am proud of her efforts to sober up. I lost two of my sons to drugs, and it goes without saying that I absolutely despise all forms of narcotics. All these circumstances, however, proved to me you can never stop being a parent. I had to step in again to care for my grandson, who has lived with us for six years. It shows that all those dreams parents have to travel the world are not practical because you never know when you will have to step in as a parental figure in someone's life.

However, I do not begrudge that I have to act as a father to my grandson, not at all. There are no feelings of anger or resentment in my heart towards him. In fact, I truly love him from the bottom of my heart.

Like I mentioned earlier, life is unpredictable, and there are moments when your plans do not pan out the way you expected them to. See, you have to be responsible in whatever role you are assigned. As a man, I knew how terribly important it is to parent your child the right way. I have been a father to my children and then their children, and I have tried to do it well. Come to think of it, being a parent is never easy, but you can only hope that you are making a difference in your children's lives. You must try and equip your blood with the right skills and tools, so they can easily traverse the murky waters of life.

Navigating Through Grief and Pain

If anything, losing my children has taught me that you must let yourself grieve. In my opinion, suppressing one's emotions is the least productive thing to do. There is bound to come a time when one's emotions get the better of them, and they explode out of anger, grief, or hurt. Instead of waiting for such a time to come, the best thing one can do is process their pain and hurt productively. Unless one consciously tries to navigate through their grief, healing cannot begin. The one thing that helped me come to terms with losing Adrian was my spiritual belief.

Getting on with your life after the death of a loved one is not as easy as people make it out to be. At every nook and crevice, seemingly mundane objects remind you of them. In fact, it would not be hyperbole to say that losing someone you love is, perhaps, the biggest challenge one has to experience in life, and frankly, I would not wish it on my enemies. Something that peeves me off quite a bit is when people interfere in someone's grieving process. In my opinion, how a person processes their grief and trauma varies from individual to individual, and there is no perfect step-by-step model one can follow to make peace with an individual's death.

As such, there is no use in telling a grieving person to just stop crying. Seriously, what would be the point of something like that? Would it help them accept whatever it is they are grieving? Obviously, no! Suppressing an emotion does not help one revert back to their normal self, not at all, and people need to make a conscious effort to cope with whatever is hurting them. It is also important to realize that there is no specific timeline for a person to completely heal. Instead, everyone processes their grief differently. While some people can make peace with their reality in a matter of weeks or months, for others, it is a completely different story, and their grieving process lasts for several years.

What matters, then, is to not rush into things. Doing so would only make the bereaving process harder than it needs to. A bit of better advice would be to be patient with yourself. Unless you are willing to give yourself time, you would not be able to fully heal, which is a fact I have learned from experience.

Life After Death

See, I firmly believe in the idea that there is life after death. I am simply not built to accept that spirits cease to exist once they experience their ultimate fate. They say that spirits love to communicate either through bots or through electrical devices. I distinctly recall an incident from my life, which holds a really special place in my heart. A few months ago, I went to take a stress test. No one accompanied me, so no one could vouch for what I experienced that day. Where I went that day, the lights around me began to flicker. Initially, I did not think much of it, but when it kept happening, I broke into laughter. If I am not wrong, I looked around and said, "Okay, boys. I know it is you, and I hope you are having a good time."

People may think I am crazy, but I know that is not true. I was in the basement of a hospital, and the nurses there escorted me to a small room. Basically, there was a machine in the room, which was supposed to take a picture of my heart. It was a perfectly beautiful room, with lights all over the place. As I was going through the routine procedures, the lights above me began to flicker, and I could swear they were flickering in tune with my heartbeat. Since it was just a stress test, I brushed it off.

After I was done, I went down to take a stress test on a treadmill, and everything went smoothly until the doctor informed me that they needed another photograph of my heart. I returned to the room with the machine, and up until this point, none of the lights there flickered. However, as the machine rotated, the same thing happened again, and the bulbs around me began flickering. By this point, my interest was piqued, but I still had not put two and two together.

Shortly afterward, I left the hospital and began walking towards my car. Sandy was there with me, and we got in the car to drive home. On the way, we started talking, and I told Sandy that I really liked the lighting in the room, where the doctors captured my heart on film. Just then, a thought began gnawing at my mind, and I asked her whether or not there was any lightning while I was in the room. To my shock, she said no. See, I was in that room twice, and both times, the bulbs started flickering as soon as the machine turned around. I do not think that was a mere coincidence, not at all.

I believe what I experienced that day was my sons communicating with me because the bond I shared with them was unbreakable. One of them spent a great deal of time with me. Initially, my ex-wife and I had him for equal amounts of time. Ultimately, though, when he turned sixteen, his mother could no longer handle him, and she sent him to live with me. While he was staying with me, he went through high school. Apart from time, we spent most of our time together, talking and doing various activities together. Even though it has been years since their death, my two boys continue to send me messages, and I simply cannot deny that. I would not stop myself from talking about it either because everything I experienced is real in my mind.

Sure, one might call me unhinged, but that does not matter. For me, my two boys are still alive. Not only do they live through me, but they communicate with me. Regardless of what people may think, there is nothing more comforting than knowing that my two boys are watching over me. Plus, all those experiences where my sons were communicating with me further endorsed my general beliefs about life.

See, there is joy in knowing that your children never leave you. Like I said before, one does not stop being a parent. Even when your son runs into the arms of another lady, they still need you. When you have a child, you try your level best to give them all those things you never got to experience in your childhood. But then, they meet someone, they get married, and then they have children. That is just how the cycle of life works, and no one can stop it from repeating itself.

At times, having a family can be overwhelming. See, when you become a parent, you do not always see eye to eye with your kid. But that is the beauty of having a family, of having children to look after. Sure, there are times when your opinions might clash with one another, but that is bound to happen. We spend so much time with our families that, at some point, we cannot help but disagree on certain themes and topics.

See, I truly believe that all of us are unique in our own ways, and when you force a bunch of distinct personalities to live together under the same roof, fights and disagreements are inevitable. In those moments, the importance of remaining cool and collected cannot be overstressed. Our words can leave a permanent mark on others, so it is better to select your words carefully instead of saying something in the heat of the moment that you might come to regret later.

But that is the beauty of family, no? Regardless of the disagreements and fights you might have with your family, they are always there for you when push comes to shove. Beautiful, isn't it? Whenever we are burdened with a particular problem, we always look to our parents, siblings, partners, and children for guidance and comfort. Here, it is important to realize that no relationship can survive as a one-way street. Reciprocation is important, and no bond can survive until and unless both parties are willing to be there for each other.

The point I am trying to make is that all those shared moments of love, affection, and adoration, as well as the times you despise each other's company, are extremely important. Those are the memories you recall when someone in your family succumbs to their mortality. I firmly believe that my sons continue to live on through me, and it comforts me to my core, knowing that they are a permanent part of my soul. They became a permanent part of my soul from the moment they were born, and I refuse to believe anything has changed after their death. To this day, I cherish the happy and sad moments we shared together, and that, my friends, is how you preserve the legacy of your loved ones.

CHAPTER 12:

THE JACKPOT OF SUCCESS

"Would you like me to give you a formula for success? It's quite simple, really: Double your rate of failure."

Thomas J. Watson

Let's make one thing perfectly clear: Money is not the measure of success. A person need not live in a fancy mansion to be deemed successful, nor do they need scores of cash sitting idly in their bank accounts. A Rolls Royce is not a symbol of success but of wealth and affluence. Unfortunately, however, most people fail to recognize that fact, especially in the 21st century, where money has become a measure of an individual's worth. Do not get me wrong! No one wants to be weighed down by financial strain, and money can definitely help an individual navigate the hurdles they encounter throughout their life. At the same time, however, it is imperative to acknowledge that wealth is not the only metric to measure a person's success.

See, the problem with such a point of view is that it reduces success to a static phenomenon, which cannot be farther from the truth. As a seventy-three-year-old man, I have interacted with a number of people, from billionaires who spend their vacations in Paris to vagrants whose nights are spent sleeping in shelter homes. From all of these experiences, I have realized one fundamental fact about life: success is a variable constant. People who deem wealth a central benchmark of one's achievements have a very reductive understanding of what it actually means to be successful. Let me elaborate.

Take a look at your surroundings. How often is it that we come across someone whose inner life is ridden with strife and contention but is overshadowed by their material possessions? I am sure most of you know someone who is doing great from a financial perspective. Not only do they have jobs where their salary package is higher than some peoples' entire life-savings, but their home is nothing short of a castle. For an outsider, such people seem to be perfectly content with their lives. The flashy cars parked in their garage further create the illusion that their lives are evocative and meaningful. But if you build a connection with them, you realize that their spiritual lives are devoid of any meaning. As such, I believe it is important to understand that such people, too, are mere humans, trying to derive whatever meaning they can with what life has been kind enough to bestow upon them.

From the dozens of people who have left a permanent impression on my life, I have realized that the worth of a person's life cannot be judged by their monetary possessions and belongings. At the risk of sounding like a broken record player, let me reiterate myself: success is not a constant phenomenon and, as such, cannot be reduced to how many cars, mansions, or bank accounts a person owns. One might ask if money is not the metric of measuring an individual's success, then what is? The answer to this question is quite simple, really. I believe that every person has a different definition of success, and as long as they fulfill the metrics sketched out by that definition, they are living a meaningful life.

For instance, take the example of an artist. Let us suppose our imaginary artist believes that their life's purpose is to produce art that can have a tangible impact on the world. Sure, they might not make a fortune with their skill. Still, as long as they are genuinely content with their profession, then none of us, in my opinion, have the right to consider their life any less meaningful than that of a businessman. If any part of them believes that they are fulfilling the purpose God endowed them with, then they cannot be regarded as anything but successful, in my opinion. Sadly, however, most people think of art as a useless endeavor in the 21st century, and children are actively forced to pursue majors they have no interest in. That I believe is a consequence of how money has come to be perceived as the only benchmark of success in our times, but I digress.

What I am trying to say is that success is a variable phenomenon, and different individuals may have different definitions of success. The renowned existentialist philosopher Jean-Paul Sartre once said,

"Existence precedes essence."

Jean-Paul Sartre

In the above quotation, Sartre tells his disciples that one need not have an essence when they are borne into the world. According to the philosopher, only after being born do we realize what our essence needs to be. Consequently, none of us can correctly assess an individual's success in life just by looking at their material wealth. Instead, we must realize that every individual is built differently and endowed with a unique purpose. Consequently, a person can be deemed successful if they manage to fulfill their purpose and get something out of their lives.

At this point, I feel the most helpful advice I can offer you is to figure out the purpose of your life, but doing so is more difficult than one expects it to be. After all, if every individual was acutely familiar with why they were born, would not the world be a bright and cheery place? Think about it for a second. I truly believe all of the wickedness and vileness that creeps around our planet is a consequence of unhappiness and dissatisfaction. One only needs to read the life story of

Hitler to realize why he committed such detestable and heinous actions during his lifetime. But if every person on Earth led a happy and meaningful life, there would be no wars, violence, chaos, and intolerance. It takes time and effort for one to undergo a long process of self-contemplation, and that is a step one cannot skip over if one wants to understand their purpose in life.

Because of Daddy John, I understood my purpose in life from a very young age. After all, I had inherited all my entrepreneurial acumen for him. If not for his help, I would be stuck somewhere, working a nine-to-five job without feeling any sense of happiness or belonging. At this point, I feel it important to detail all of the pieces of advice I wish someone would have given me when I kickstarted my professional career. All of these things helped me convert my entrepreneurial vision into a reality.

1. Go With Your Gut

In my experience, the first step you can take to seek your life's purpose is to go with your instinct, even if it compels you to step out of your comfort zone. See, had I never trusted my gut and left the shipyard, there is a high probability that I would still be working there, breaking my back for menial pay. Like I mentioned earlier, it was sort of like a custom for the men in our family to spend their entire lives toiling in a shipyard. Both my father and grandfather had devoted a significant chunk of their lives working there. I, however, could not bring myself to believe that my purpose in life was to serve as labor-power in a shipyard. That just did not make sense to me. Maybe, it was true in the case of my father and my grandfather, but I cannot really say. The only thing I knew at the time was that working in a boatyard was not the life I envisioned for myself.

Come to think of it, leaving the shipyard to go work at IBM was the best decision I ever made. At the time, it felt as if I was turning my back on my family, but now, I am glad for following my gut. As one can imagine, my parents were strictly against my decision. One day, my dad even took me to the doctor because I no longer wanted to be involved in the shipyard. Let me make one thing clear, however. I do not have grudges towards my parents. See, I was born in an underprivileged family, and as such, both my mother and father did not want to take any unnecessary risks that might have aggravated their financial trouble. It only makes sense that they never pushed themselves out of their comfort zones to build a better and more meaningful life.

On the other hand, I was willing to risk it all for my future. The more I think of it, the more natural it seems for my parents to stop me from joining IBM. In their minds, they must have worried about what would happen if my new job did not pan out the way I had expected it to. At times, however, you must stop yourself from looking so far ahead into the future. None of us have any idea whether or not we will be alive tomorrow. Plus, life is unpredictable, and at times, even our most thought-out plans cannot escape the contingency of our existence. Hence, I believe that you must follow your gut without worrying about the future. Sure, it is beneficial to plan what you want to do with your life, but as soon as an opportunity presents itself, you must grab it by the horns. If you waste too much time trying to predict the future, that opportunity might disappear, and then, you will be left with nothing but regrets.

I cannot overstress the importance of trusting your gut, as it may be the only thing capable of helping you circumvent the adversities that plague your life. Looking back at it, had I not pushed myself out of the safe confines of my comfort zone and joined IBM, only God knows where I would be today. I might still have been stuck at the shipyard, living a life that was devoid of any meaning and purpose.

2. Resilience is Key

Let me begin by narrating a short poem for you,

"When things go wrong, as they sometimes will,

When the road you're trudging seems all uphill,

When the funds are low, but the debts are high,

And you want to smile, but you have to sigh,

When care is pressing you down a bit...

Rest if you must, but don't you quit!

Life is queer with its twists and turns,

As every one of us sometimes learns,

And many failures turn about

When we might have won had we stuck it out.

Don't give up though the pace seems slow...

You may succeed with another blow.

Often the struggler has given up

When he might have captured the victor's cup;

And he learned too late when the night came down,

How close he was to the golden crown.

Success is failure turned inside out...

And you can never tell how close you are

It may be near when it seems so far.

So stick to the fight when you're hardest hit

It's when things seem worst that you must not quit.

~

Edgar A. Guest

There is no shortcut to success in life. Hard work, resilience, consistency are only some of the traits needed for one to convert their vision into a reality. The bottomline is that an individual cannot expect to lead a meaningful existence without blood, sweat, and tears. See, life will not serve the treasures and riches it has to offer you if you are unwilling to put in any effort towards the goals and milestones you have set for yourself.

Life is not a bed of roses but one laden with thorns and prickles. Do not get me wrong. I do not mean that the nature of life is inherently violent and sadistic, not at all. Instead, think of life as a demanding instructor who tests you at every twist and turns. In the end, however, you realize that you have learned more from that professor than anyone else. Similarly, the trials and tribulations one encounters in life are nothing more than a mere test. As long as you remain determined and committed to your aims and ambitions, life will present you with the fruits of your efforts on a golden platter.

In other words, you have to try and beat life in its own games. There will be times when all of your efforts and hard work will go down the drain, and you will have no choice to start again from scratch. The decision you make at this point will determine whether or not you will lead a meaningful and successful life.

At times when life knocks you down, you must muster up the strength to get back on your feet, continue to work and stay focused.

Traversing through the murky waters of life is similar to riding a bicycle. If you fall off, you have no choice to get back on it and hope you get it right the next time around. In today's world, people tend to see failure as an indication of an individual's stupidity, but that cannot be further from the truth, in my opinion. I firmly believe that failure is the essential ingredient for success. Until and unless one has struck rock-bottom, they cannot realize their mistakes and rectify them.

Here, I cannot help but recall an old photo of Jeff Bezos back in the old days of Amazon. The photo was captured in a dingy, old room, and that version of Bezos did not look half as polished and professional as he does today. But that is the thing, isn't it? People always tend to focus on the end result. Nobody realizes what Bezos had to do to get over the hurdles and obstacles that blocked his path to success. Nobody knows the number of nights caffeine served as a substitute for his sleep, and nobody appreciates how many times he had to fail before becoming a billionaire.

I do not know of any business models that did not fail at least once or twice. Many successful entrepreneurs have even filed for bankruptcy multiple times because they simply could not afford the expenses for running their business, but that does not matter in the least. What matters is when life knocked them down, they had the gall to dust themselves off and start all over again. See, leading a successful, meaningful, and happy life requires commitment, hard work, and determination, all of which test one's resilience to the core. The point is failure is not a sign of weakness. Instead, it is the stimulant one needs to reinvent themselves according to their goals and ambitions.

Take my example, for instance. The first time I applied to IBM, my application was rejected. I could have simply given up, but that experience lit a fire inside my heart. Deep down, I knew I could make it there, so instead of quitting, I applied to the company once more, only to get rejected again. But even as a young boy, I realized that there is value in failure. After all, failure is necessary for one to devise new ways and strategies to fulfill their aims.

Consequently, instead of backing out, I kept my chin up high. It took me thirteen attempts to get my application accepted by IBM, after which I was finally offered a job by the company. Needless to say, I learned a lot from this experience. First and foremost, each time my application was rejected, I understood where I was going wrong. As such, I had no choice but to build myself up from scratch into a person even a corporation like IBM would be proud to call its employee. Secondly, the age-old saying that perseverance pays off finally made sense to me.

In my experience, we need to be consistent in our efforts, and as such, we must be the Sisyphus of our own lives. According to Greek mythology, Sisyphus was the king of Corinth, a city in Greece, where he practiced a reign of tyranny to maintain his rule. After he died, he was taken to the underworld. However, before he could be punished for his crimes, he managed to chain up Thanatos, the personification of death, due to which death could no longer perform its function, and no more humans died. Sisyphus's actions greatly upset Ares, the God of war, who no longer enjoyed waging war on the planet as they would last for years without bloodshed or violence. Only after Ares freed Thanatos did things on Earth go back to normal, but that was not the end of Sisyphus's fondness for deceit and trickery.

After he died for the second time, the King tricked Hades's wife, Persephone, into letting him travel back to the realm of the living, so he could convince his wife to perform all of the necessary rituals and sacrifices. When Persephone finally obliged his request, Sisyphus never returned to the underworld and lived a new, rejuvenated life. But as the saying goes, all good things come to an end. Zeus, the King of the Greek gods, was tired of Sisyphus's knack for cheating death, and when the latter died once again, he was condemned to everlasting punishment. According to the legend, Zeus condemned Sisyphus to roll a boulder up a steep hill, but whenever the rock neared the hill's edge, it would roll back down, and Sisyphus would have to repeat his actions all over again. In this manner, the once terrible king of Corinth was cursed to a lifetime of toil and drudgery.

For most people, the tale of Sisyphus is a stark reminder of how one cannot escape from their ultimate fate, i.e., the unyielding scythe of the grim reaper. That, however, is not true in my case. From my perspective, Sisyphus is a symbol of all one needs to lead a meaningful life. See, even though he knows that all of his efforts will be in vain, he never gives up the mantle of hope and optimism. Every time the boulder rolls back down the hill, Sisyphus starts working from scratch, hoping and praying that the end result would be different this time around. That, in my opinion, is how one should approach life as well.

Regardless of how many times life knocks us down, we must keep going. We must dust ourselves off before getting up again and continuing our journey towards success, hoping to achieve whatever goals and milestones we have set for ourselves. Only then can we truly fulfill our purpose and lead a life full of meaning, happiness, and success. Giving up will yield nothing. After all, you never know how close you might be to the one-yard line, and quitting then would be an utter waste of your time and efforts. As the saying goes,

"Success seems to be largely a matter of hanging on after others have let go."

William Feather

1. Change is Constant

The only constant in life is change, and that, my friends, is the bottom line. As we go through life, our needs, wants, and desires evolve over time. Think about it for a minute, will you? See, when we are young, innocent, and naïve, something as mundane as candy is enough to make us happy. When we transition into adults, however, our minds come to be occupied with hundreds of responsibilities, from finding a stable source of income to building a good life for our children. But such a change is only natural, no? After all, as the world evolves, so do we. Otherwise, we are left behind by time, a force beyond our control.

For any aspiring entrepreneurs, mark my words: time does not wait for anyone. If you are not ready for an opportunity, someone else will be, and you will be left with nothing but regret. In the 21st century, in particular, change is visible all around us.

Every day, thousands of technologies are rendered obsolete by new and emerging automatons. The world as we know it has fundamentally changed, and today's generation is living in an extremely fast-paced world.

Sadly, however, most people fail to accept such a reality. It is not uncommon for one to come across someone with a strong nostalgia for the past. After all, how often does one find a person talking about how easy things used to be back in the good old days? As someone whose candle is about to be burnt out, I can say from experience that such a point of view is not viable in the long run. Sure, the past might have been better than the present in a hundred ways, but that does not mean we should keep ruminating on how things used to be.

I have been an entrepreneur for more than half of my life, during which I have had to alter my approach to business several times. Come to think of it, had I not been receptive to those changes, none of my businesses would have survived. Back when I established my first business, Quality Microsystems, in Alabama, things were quite different from today. At the time, laser printers were almost unheard of, and it did not take me long to think up novel ways to capitalize on them. With my help, Quality Microsystems introduced a desktop laser printer, which immediately became a success. The selling price of the laser printer was approximately two thousand dollars, and hundreds of clients flocked in the market to buy our product.

I could have stopped then and there, but I realized that sooner or later, the market craze for laser printers was bound to run out of steam. See, the mind of an entrepreneur never ceases to let go of an opportunity, and soon after, I joined another company, Laser Connection. There, my knack for innovation helped me introduce toner cartridges. Laser printers equipped with toner cartridges became so famous in the American market, increasing our profits significantly. Because of its success, Laser Connection soon expanded to Huntsville, Alabama, where I assumed the role of an incubator for emerging businesses.

I continued to hone my knowledge and skills, and by the time I laid the foundations of my third business, I had grown accustomed to reinventing myself. My responsibilities were engineering hardware for motherboards placed inside laser printers, and frankly, I learned quite a lot from that experience. It is only because of my ability to attune myself in line with the changes taking place in society at large that, today, I am the Chief Operating Officer and Chairman of two public companies, one of which is soon to become a spearhead in the technology industry. Not only that, but I am also the joint-owner of somewhere around sixty-four other companies. To this day, I believe none of my success would have been possible had I not adapted to the changes taking place in the market.

Acclimating yourself to change is not only important for entrepreneurs, but it is a great piece of advice for everyone to follow. Even at my age, I try my best to become familiar with the fluctuations occurring in my surroundings. In fact, one of my favorite pastimes is to acclimate myself to new and emerging technologies. Just because I am old does not mean I should patiently wait for death to escort me back to where I came from, not at all. As William Arthur Ward said,

"The pessimist complains about the wind; the optimist expects it to change; the realist adjusts the sails."

William Arthur Ward

If you want to be successful, you must mimic the realist who recalibrates his sails. Only then can you hope to live a life that is full to the brim with meaning, success, and happiness in the long run. Otherwise, time will slip right out of the palms of your hands, and you will have no choice but to be left behind by forces beyond your control. That is all I have to say.

2. Cherish the Ones Around You

"It didn't matter how big our house was; it mattered that there was love in it."

Peter Buffet

Throughout the seven and a half decades I have been alive, my friends and family have repeatedly helped me navigate my personal and professional life. I feel no shame in admitting that it would have been next to impossible for me to be where I am today without the care and support of my loved ones. See, each of us is unique, but perhaps the only commonality we do share is that we all crave the company of fellow humans. Whether or not you are an introvert does not really matter because there comes the point in every individual's life where they yearn for both physical and emotional intimacy.

From the time we are born to the moment we draw in our last breath, we are surrounded by other humans. As such, no matter how hard one tries to portray themselves as a lone wolf, the bottom line is we would not be able to survive without cooperation and compromise. One need not look too far back into history to understand how humans are mutually dependent on one another.

In a famous lecture delivered by Margaret Mead, a cultural anthropologist, she was asked by one of her students about the first sign of civilization. Most of the audience present in the auditorium expected Mead to reference ancient artifacts, such as tools, weapons, crafts, and religious figures, in her answer. Instead, her response was relatively straightforward. According to her, the first sign of civilization was a fractured femur, whose existence dated back to almost fifteen thousand years ago. Analysis of the femur showed that it had once been fractured but had healed since then.

See, it typically takes six weeks for a person to recover from a broken femur, and in the animal kingdom, suffering from a leg injury means an irreversible death sentence. After all, one cannot fend for themselves with a broken leg, and in most cases, they become a meal for other wild predators. According to the anthropologist, discovering a healed femur meant that another human had stayed behind with the injured person and helped them recover. Profound, isn't it? The purpose of narrating this incident is to show how cooperation and mutual support form the basis of any human civilization.

As such, we cannot expect to navigate the trials and tribulations of life without relying on the love and affection of our friends and family. It is a sad fact of our reality that people have stopped giving relationships the value they deserve. Think about it for a moment.

Isn't it true that the only times we tend to really open up to our friends and family is when we feel distressed or when a particular problem is bothering the peace of our mind?

But when things are going well, we rarely play a supportive role in another person's life. In today's world, it is effortless to get distracted. All of us are already burdened with several responsibilities, from securing a well-paying job to getting suitable grades to get enrolled in a world-class university. As such, it is easy for a person to direct all their attention towards a rather mundane task instead of actively doing their due diligence towards their loved ones.

I believe the same happened to me in my earlier marriages. When I married my first wife, Patricia, I was confident that she was the right person for me. In my mind, I believed that we would always stay together and build a beautiful little family, and when it would be time for us to bid farewell to the world, we would not be burdened by any regrets. Little did I know how wrong I was. Soon into my marriage, I was recruited by IBM, which gave my professional career a kickstart. Apparently, I was good at doing my job, so my employers sent me to France, Germany, Italy, etc., to handle some clients and projects. During this period, Patricia and I were also blessed with our first child.

Sadly, however, my relatively newfound success at IBM helped me realize my true potential, and I got so engrossed in my work that I began to overlook my familial obligations. That basically meant that Patricia was left alone to care for the house, which obviously irked her. Because of this and several other reasons, our relationship gradually disintegrated until we decided to separate. There was nothing I could do to make things rights, and frankly, a part of me did not want to. Like I mentioned earlier, Patricia and I shared a powerful connection, but our bond was more platonic than romantic. Plus, we did not have many similar interests, and our personalities did not match in the slightest.

It took me some time to realize that Patricia and I were not well-matched to be each other's partners, which made the entire idea of getting divorced a bit more palatable.

Here, I want to stress the importance of letting go of people. Sure, it might sound absurd to disassociate yourself from your relationships, but that is the entire point! A healthy relationship would never hold you back from unleashing your true potential. But if that is not the case, then one needs to deliberate on whether or not they want to continue putting effort into such a relationship.

See, a relationship should be mutually beneficial for both the involved parties. Not only should your partner be there to provide you with emotional and physical support, but you also need to do the same for them. Any relationship that works as a one-way street is bound to end up in failure. Looking back at my first marriage, I cannot help but feel somewhat responsible for how it ended. Maybe if I had been more diligent in fulfilling my responsibilities as a loving husband and father, things would have turned out differently. Similarly, had Patricia been more receptive to my entrepreneurial spirit, we might still have been together. At the end of the day, however, I am glad that we decided to split as it helped me realize how much I still needed to grow as a person.

What I am trying to say is that keep your loved ones close to you. Life is short, and you do not want to be someone who lets their relationship disintegrate into nothingness just to attain some form of rudimentary success. In fact, it would not be hyperbole to say that having a strong support system in the form of a family is in itself a kind of success that most people fail to achieve in their lives. Before you strive to become a better businessman, strive to become a better partner, sibling, parent, etc. Like I keep saying, no one remembers you for your worldly possessions, but for whether or not you were there for them in their time of need. In the words of Richard Branson,

"However important business is, family always comes first."

If there is one thing I want you to take away from this chapter, money is not the metric for success. As long as you focus on fulfilling your purpose in life, you will lead a life packed with meaning and success. Trust your gut regardless of what others might say, and never ever stop trying. If you fail, then so be it! Learn from your failures, so the next time you try something, you do not repeat the same mistakes.

Be innovative in everything you do. The world around us is in constant flux, and we cannot hope to achieve anything in life if we are stuck in the past. Finally, and perhaps most importantly, acknowledge the fact that life is short. All of us will ultimately die, and the scary part is we will never know when that might happen. Hold your loved ones close, hug them, and tell them you love them. In the end, none of your success would amount to anything if you fail to make a difference in another person's life.

CHAPTER 13:

FIFTH'S A CHARM

Do you ever feel like you are at a loss of guidance in your life? If your answer is yes, I have good news for you – it happens to *everyone*! As human beings, we tend to fall in and out of the circle of support as we find ourselves in different situations. But that is how life goes. Sometimes we get to the bottom to get to the top, and sometimes when we reach the top, the next step takes us to the bottom to help us rise. We do not understand these intricacies in life when we are young, but they are crucial to keeping us going.

When I was younger, too, I often questioned the reason for my fall or failure in the first place. I never let it get to me enough to hold me back, but I always pondered how it helped me at that moment. My mentors have always taught me never to fear moments when things don't work your way, and that is precisely the advice I will give you through my words and my book. My life's journey is all about getting my experiences out of myself and into a form you can benefit from. That is the purest way of learning, is it not? Passing on lessons and experiences?

I was once just a little, average boy. I never thought I would be a billionaire a couple of decades down the line. God knows I had not planned to accumulate money in my bank accounts. As I grew up, my circumstances built a filter in my perception that helped me identify a gap in the market and actualize the situation. Whether it be killing chickens for a living on Christmas or making a sliver's worth of profit selling buns and butter, I saw every opportunity as a chance to grow. When you seek internal growth, you attract and pick challenges that strengthen your skills and sometimes even rid you of your weaknesses.

Life is a series of unfortunate yet fortunate events waiting for you to (wo)man up and dig deeper. On the surface level, everything is tough, but it is the grind that will keep you going. If I reflect on my life so far, I started off as a boy who worked in the shipyards to the man today who works in different capacities for sixty-four companies and co-owns two others. The journey to this point has been full of more obstacles than successes, and that is pretty much the defining point of my life. We are human beings who have no manual to get by in life. All we get are first-hand experiences, heartbreaks from failures, and sometimes even disappointments that propel us forward. In the end, it is not about how successful you have been but what you make of those successes.

When you bring your mind and your body together on your missions, you achieve things you never thought of. Ideas that seemed far away come closer, and their feasibility becomes much more positive. When you keep going in the face of adversity, you prove to yourself and the world around you that you are willing to do whatever it takes to get ahead. The most successful people in the world are those that don't settle and keep moving. We are often inspired by success stories but unwilling to put in the work required to make those stories work. Some people think luck makes the world go round when really, it is hard work that gets you from where you are to where you want to go.

"Success is the ability to go from one failure to another with no loss of enthusiasm."

Winston Churchill

The best way to get through your difficulties is to face them. If there is one absolute lesson I have learned in life, it is that you cannot avoid any problems, and there are no shortcuts in life. Learning is always a time-taking process. It comes with a curve but leads to linear, maybe even exponential, levels of success. We can either embrace our fate to make an exceptional journey out of it, or we can fight our circumstances and lose everything in the process. The human brain will always trick you into taking the safest route to do things. The evolutionary perspective states that you are naturally inclined to stay in a comfort zone, protecting the human mind and body from harmful and foreign experiences. However, it is important to know that mediocracy only results in achieving the average and known. To get out there and make a name for yourself, the nature of work you put in needs to be unique and even unusual if need be.

If I did not go through what I did, I would not be writing this book today. There are moments where I have been proud of myself and other times where I questioned myself for doing something that seemed absolutely insane. However, I never backed down. I kept using my failures to build stairs under my own two feet, moving forward with everything I knew. Who would have thought that a Scottish kid out of a small town would be one day making a difference in the lives of so many people? I certainly did not. But I had an instinct that I just had to follow. From tagging along with my Daddy John on his adventures and learning from his business acumen to making strategic business decisions as a board member, my life's story is here to help all those struggling to get to where they want. I am here to tell you that it is all possible. You will get to where you want as long as you are willing to put in the effort. At first, the path may seem shaky and blurred. You may seem like your hard work is not materializing, but the fact of the matter is that all good things take time, and you have to be patient. Some tasks you will do to make ends meet, while others are meant to fulfill your soul and purpose in life. You may not always find the two goals in one unless you are an extraordinary human being, but let's face it, we all need recreational activity outside of work to get by. Your recreational activity could be your hobby, such as reading up on the stock market, spending time at the library on the weekends giving yourself a history lesson, or simply meeting up with friends to discuss an upcoming business idea till you launch it. The key is that you keep yourself occupied and utilize your potential to its fullest. I probably would not have been here if I did not get the push that I needed from the get-go. But I also understand that not everyone is lucky enough to experience this privilege. Hence, I am here for all those who feel like they have no one to rely on or go to for guidance. The way I see it, life is a long journey. We all need someone to get by, and sometimes, it might get difficult to spot opportunities that are meant to turn your life around, but with the right guidance and lens, you should be able to do what others are struggling with.

If I were to condense the teachings I have obtained in life, I would much rather categorize them by the people I have come across as opposed to the lessons people have taught me. You see, as an empath, I remember what people make me feel, and those feelings trigger the lessons. In turn, I learned from them. The best way to hold someone in high regard is to keep them in your prayers, wishing the best to them and helping them if they ever need it. People may forget what you said or what you did, but no one forgets how you make them feel. Hence, the best way to be remembered is with memory and in a positive light as opposed to someone people want to avoid.

Henry Bonar

My father, one of my greatest sources of inspiration, really set a foundation of discipline and mannerisms in my life. Growing up, I would see him work hard to provide whatever he could for us. Sure, we lived in a small town, in a small house, but his efforts were large enough to provide us with exactly what we needed. He never gave up in the face of difficulty, persevering through tough times to be the best husband and father he could be. As an entrepreneur today, I would gladly say that I got my will to keep going because of my father. If it were not for him, I would not have known where I was wrong, especially in my personal life.

At first, when he would talk to me about my relationships, I would brush off his advice thinking, 'We are a different generation' or 'He does not know how the world today works,' something you might have thought when you picked up this book and realized that I am well into my seventh decade. But only half of that fact is true. They might not be up to speed with how things currently work, but they know the origin of the people around them. Their experience can sometimes speak volumes and play a major role in helping us survive in this world, even if we are not willing to listen to what our fathers have to say.

Margaret Bonar

If I were to pick a person who shaped my soft skills in life, I would say it was my mother. She was a kind, resilient woman who made the most of what my father could provide for us. I had never seen her complain in the time that we all lived under one roof as a family, and I know, for a fact, that she is not the kind of woman anyway. She came from a humble background, in the same town I grew up in, and instilled the same qualities within her kids; probably the reason I have never run after money in my life.

My mother loved knitting and made sweaters for us out of wool to keep us warm during the winters. The simple woman she was, she stuck to the pattern she knew, and all our sweaters turned out to be more or less the same. Even when I asked her to change the knitting fashion, she would say, "Oh, son! Stick to your knitting, and you will be okay." Back then, I did not really understand what she meant, but her words opened me up to accept the ideologies and processes of others.

Even today, when someone comes to me with a great idea that I know nothing about, I let them stick to it without making too many changes to it. I put myself in a situation to learn, just like I did about my mother and her habits, without being preachy or trying to control the situation. We rise by letting those around us grow as well, or else the weight on our shoulders becomes too much to carry everyone else.

My mother's simplicity reflected in the way that she made our house a home, always friendly with her kids, ensuring to treat us like people. Even when I came up with the most absurd ideas to start businesses, she never discouraged me. In fact, she would laugh when I would go up to her with my silly ideas, never discouraging me from doing anything. She would leave me with a small piece of advice every time. Her advice to stay humble in order to be content with life will always stick with me through and through. I think it is one mantra I have kept close to my heart that keeps me down-to-earth to this day.

Daddy John

If I have not spoken about my Daddy John already, I would like to summarize this great guy and his impact on my life once again. I started my first business under his influence, and to this day, I still use his teachings in my life and entrepreneurial journey. If it was not for him, I would not be here. There is no doubt about it. Daddy John is a god sent to me. I wish everyone gets a mentor and support system like him.

One of the most important lessons Daddy John's company taught me was that it is good to have a plan, but it is not all you need to move ahead. If you are not paying attention to the plan, you are going to lose the entire idea. Once again, it is like walking a tight rope with a pole in your hand. While the idea originates in your head and is manifested through your actions, the pole is what will balance your idea and the work put into it. You need to keep this pole at equilibrium by experimenting with your idea at one end, and revisiting the plan, and updating it with your learning on the other. Fundamentally, I think that is what will make your plan successful. Revising and updating your idea with the learning that you receive as you go.

I saw Daddy John maintain a balance between his personal and professional life. He had a great relationship with his wife and would often visit us on his weekends, where we would spend time together. Although it personally took me a while to understand how to strike a balance, a part of me knows that without the presence of this man in my life, I probably never would have gotten to this point. God knows I would be single forever. Nevertheless, it happened, and on most days, that is what I am grateful for.

Just as I put in the effort and watched my businesses and entrepreneurship skills manifest, when I started to reflect on my relationships, I detected a pattern and began working on correcting it. I have big dreams for my company Dalrada Corporation and plan on taking it to NASDAQ. All in all, my success and planning today would not exist without the teachings of my Daddy John.

Jimmy Miller

If I were to define Jimmy Miller in a sentence, I would say that he is the best secret teacher I have ever had. You see, the thing about a person like him was that he never altered his energy to match someone else's. He maintained his own vibe and personality, and hence, he attracted those who withheld positivity inside them. Jimmy Miller lit up the place, and everyone knew that. A day without him would be so dull that it would feel like something wonderful had died.

People on the floor would greet Jimmy with glee and enthusiasm. Honestly, a guy like that is hard to come by and even harder to forget. Like I have already mentioned before, you may not always remember what people do or say, but you always remember how they make or made you feel. In Jimmy's case, all three are applicable because the feeling of care and understanding that follows after someone asks you about your day is contagious. You ought to carry around the emotion with you. Jimmy had set this trend of compassion and care all around, and everyone started following his lead, myself included. I saw everyone's eyes light up just as we heard Jimmy Miller's laugh getting closer, an indication he was close by. Everyone wanted to be part of the positivity, and I try to carry a part of Jimmy inside me wherever I go.

Summarizing everything I have said so far, I have five important tips to follow to get through your life in a happy, healthy way. Of course, these are a combination of personal and professional tips alike, but these tips are a good place to start for those looking to lead happy and healthy lives. These rules are neither exhaustive nor are they definite. You can try your own combination of items that have worked for you and maybe learn something new from your life's journey because, after all, we are all put here to grow.

CHAPTER 14:

NEW BEGINNINGS

Not all the fairy scenes of youth,

Of days and years gone by,

Which faithful memory wakes to light,

The soul can satisfy.

Nor all the present joys we share,

However high they rise,

Health, wealth, or friends or all combined

Nor aught beneath the skies,

Can satisfy the craving mind;

It sighs for something more

Than earth can give, or Heaven bestows,

Here on this desert shore.

It looks away and feeds on hope

Of fairer scenes to come,

Some safe, some blissful resting-place

Some surer, happier home.

Take hope, from man, you take his all,

The past, the present dies,--

He cannot live when broken off,

His outlet to the skies,

The hope of heaven is more enjoined,

Then earth's realities:

These fade and vanish from the sight,

But hope, it never dies.

~

Hope

by Benjamin Hine

Strengthening any relationship or event in life requires working towards it with your heart and soul. Your relationships will fail, and your businesses will leave empty if you do things half-heartedly. Not because you did not put in enough effort, but mostly because you did not figure yourself out enough to know what to go after. People often take the wrong job that pays well or marry the wrong person who makes them happy during the first few months of the relationship because they do not anticipate the hard work that needs to be put in once the honeymoon phase of the process is over. That's when everything starts to fall apart and fades away. Businesses might do well in the beginning in terms of profit and money-making, and your marriage may seem happy because you do not have much to compare it to. But as time passes by, things require time and effort to be sustained.

Think about yourself. The older you grow, the more your taste and develop your flavor. You eat much more complex food, wear different outfits, and make much more difficult decisions. Basically, you move forward and evolve. Similarly, when you are involved with people, whether personally or professionally, you need to ensure that you grow with them and vice versa, or you will end up outgrowing them. This is why you sometimes need to leave your hometown, or even your comfort zone, as you grow up, to grow as a person and as an adult.

When I was younger, I worked around the clock. I had no time in the world to share it with the people who were a major part of my life. I literally moved with the hands of the clock as if I had 12 hours in a day instead of 24. I lost four wives to a routine that was so hectic; it barely gave me time to focus on anything else. Now when I look in hindsight, I realize that I should have made myself available. I had kids who I tried to keep with me, but they, too, grew up and now do their own thing. But that is just the way that life works, isn't it? You can either try to maintain the life status you once had because it is comfortable, or you can plunge yourself into newness till it feels like home to you. Since we have been together, my wife Sandy has taught me that it is okay to just listen sometimes. You do not need to have the answer sometimes, and you need to trust your spouse when they have an opinion, something that is entirely new to me. Now, I don't run out of the house every chance I get because I listen to Sandy when she tells me something I do not understand, and I try to work on it sincerely and earnestly. As human beings, we all want to be heard, loved, and accepted; sometimes, without any questions asked or solutions suggested.

Before I met my wife Sandy, I had given hope to marriage and relationships. I had lived a full life, had kids, made money, and had enough to get me through the rest of my life.

I did not know what I was missing out on until I met her, the perfect woman I have come across, although she has her own set of weaknesses and insecurities. When I started building with Sandy, and even to this day, I have slowly started to understand why none of my previous relationships have worked, and it makes sense. I am grateful this happened when it did because everything before her taught me how to treat her right. Sandy is a tough woman who knows what she wants in her life. She is also a businesswoman who has been in the market for the past twenty-five years. I commend her for her strength as she has only been married once in her life. Everything in her life she has, she built on her own. She has wonderful kids that she brought up. One of my most favorite qualities is the fact that she is put together. She is balanced and even-tempered. I would even go as much as to say that she is my voice of reason when I lose sight of things.

Sandy is part German and part French, or that is what she told me when we initially met. I still laugh at that moment because I now know that she lied. I never know why but every time we discuss this, we laugh because she is, in fact, forty-eight percent Scottish and grew up in the same county as me. Small world, huh? Who would have thought that the person I went around the world to find was right there, only a few miles away from me all this time? But that is the funny thing about fate and the universe. You can miss something that is right between your two hands and catch something traveling toward you a hundred miles an hour. It is all a matter of being in the right place at the right time. Some things are out of your control, and for days when you come across events that make you realize this fact, patience and understanding should be your best friends to walk you through that tightrope.

Sandy has been with me through some of the toughest times in my life. We have stuck together through the death of our two children, another one of them struggling with drugs, who we are hoping to get cleaned soon. When I struggle through my businesses and tough corporate decisions, Sandy chimes in with her expertise and tries to guide me just as much as I help her. Through my relationship with Sandy, I have also learnt that men often lack the capacity to simply listen. Sometimes, it is not about providing a solution or an answer to the problem. Women usually know how to get through things; sometimes, all they need is a partner to hear them vent, just as men do. I remember one time when Sandy was upset and was speaking to me about how bad her day had been. Naturally, being a problem fixer, I tried to offer her solutions which only agitated her.

"Well, you have the facts, and you know the solution to the problem," I told her.

"Right now, I don't want to fix it. I just want you to listen to me," she replied.

As difficult as it is for me not to provide a solution, I held myself back and slowly learned to give in to the fact that she just needed to be held. Emotionally, physically, and even mentally sometimes. Human beings just want to know that they are not alone. We can figure out our solutions most times. We are not business entities with no rationality that will fall without absolute human intervention but fragile beings who want to be pampered.

I have developed a system where at the start of a conversation, when I feel like Sandy wants to get a load off her chest, I simply ask her what she wants.

"Honey, do you want me to just listen? Or do you want me to offer my input?"

And she will often just say, "I just want you to listen." And for the next few minutes, all I do is offer a hearing ear and open arms for her to vent into. It could be the color of the sky, or the cat or the dog, or even the paint on the wall. Once she has let go of what is bothering her, she becomes level-headed enough to make other sound decisions.

My relationship with my wife has taught me even more things about myself than I thought. A marriage is supposed to be balanced financially, mentally, and emotionally. We are taught that if you are a man, you are not allowed to cry and that if you are a woman, your first priority is your children. But that is not true. Human beings are flexible and capable of many things. Tying them down to one goal and objective limits their creativity, putting a cap on their capacity to their abilities. Because I was so focused on building a business and making money for sustenance all these years, I missed out on family time and having fulfilling personal relationships. Sure, I have a good relationship with my ex-wives to this day, but I did have to go through my fair share of trouble to get where I am today.

I tell people I am semi-retired, meaning I go to work only a few days a week. I work from home, per my own convenience, maybe two days a week, and physically go to the office the other three days. I hang out on my boat on days I feel like getting out of the house and working remotely. Some days, I am more productive, while other days, I just hang out with people to know what is going on in their lives. I can assure you that as long as there is a balance between what is personal and professional, things will work out. And they will work out in your favor, even though you are trying to make other people stable in their lives. You see, at this point, supporting people and guiding them is what helps me get out of bed every day. I think about people who are stuck in a rut, who have lost hope in love and work, who think that they won't reach anywhere in life, and who think that it's the end of their world. That's when I feel an instant urge to tell them that it's not. Even my wife, Sandy, admires this quality of mine. She loves how driven I am about making the lives of those around me better and confessed it to me quite a few times. I want to tell the whole world that it is possible to support each other's goals without losing your own identity or causing them to lose theirs. We work in many social circles. Hence, managing certain personalities around certain people is the key. Give people the time and space they need to figure things out and see the magic happening.

We are fathers and mothers, daughters and sons, brothers and sisters, and friends and lovers, trying to get by in a world where there is no set manual given to us to do things. We are all trying our best and in the best possible way. Trust me when I say this. The least we can do is be kinder to each other, understanding that life is tough, so you don't have to be.

"Enjoy your life, for everything else comes and goes till there is nothing left."

Brian Bonar